Wind River Trails

A hiking and fishing guide to the
many trails and lakes of the

The University of Utah Press
Salt Lake City

YOUR LAND AND MINE

May you always camp where waters run clear
Within serene valleys of flowers and shade,
Where well trod trails of friendship meet
And your kindness and grace never fade.

Where solitude's found and shared with another,
A friendship is formed with a long lost soul;
Where dreams are all sacred, joys are all new,
The world is much brighter, a future to unfold.

Where mountain tops rise and the eagle doth soar,
The glaciers are eternal and the bighorns roam;
Where man is a visitor in his trespassing way,
But the pica has made it his solitary home.

For these depths of mountains we so often yearn,
Yet man seldom wanders where nature controls;
Where man becomes lost in the midst of his dreams
Only God can be guide for so many lost souls.

Finis Mitchell

The Defiance House Man colophon is a registered trademark
of the University of Utah Press. It is based upon a four-foot-tall,
Ancient Puebloan pictograph (late PIII) near Glen Canyon, Utah.

Cover photo: Square Top Mountain
over Green River Lakes
by Finis Mitchell

Finis Mitchell, "Man O' the Mountains"

A short hike 71 years ago was the beginning of a long career in wilderness living for Finis Mitchell of Rock Springs, Wyoming. He has scaled 244 peaks, including four times to the top of Gannett Peak, the highest mountain in the state. A vigorous supporter of wilderness, the mountain man pours out his philosophy at meetings and slide shows with amazing attention to detail. He has taken 105,345 pictures as a hobby and uses them in his slide shows to show people their own public lands. He has drawn on his vast experience in the Wind Rivers to describe in this guide book the trails, routes, wildlife, glaciers, 4,000 lakes and 800 miles of streams in Wyoming's fabulous two and a quarter million acre Wind River Range.

Editor

3

CONTENTS

ENTRANCES

TRAILS AND ROUTES

MAPS

AUTOBIOGRAPHY

I came to Wyoming from Missouri with my parents with a span of mules, a wagon and a cow. We arrived April 26, 1906 at the foot of the great 2-1/4-million-acre Wind River Range. Our worldly possessions were in that wagon and on our backs.

While with my father in October 1909 hunting elk for food, he started me to climbing mountains. I've never quit. Since that October day so long ago, I have climbed 244 peaks and still climb every summer. The range was our back yard. In 1920 I began taking pictures as a hobby with my climbing so I could show people where I'd been and what was there in our National Forests.

I went to Rock Springs and began working for the U.P.R.R. June 4, 1923, but was laid off March 4, 1930 due to the big depression.

6

Mitchells Fishing Camp, 1932

I had gotten married June 4, 1925. When they laid me off I went back to the mountains to trap because there were no jobs, even for the beggars.

At that time the great Wind River Range had been used only for sheep and cattle grazing for some 90 years, and they had fought vicious battles over free range. Because there simply was no way to earn a living, in June 1930 my wife and I bought a tent, borrowed horses and saddles and started our Mitchell's Fishing Camp in the Big Sandy Openings. We followed the sheep wagon road to its end and set up our tent.

When we set up our fishing camp on Mud Lake that June in 1930, there were only about five lakes that had fish in them. These were all cutthroat trout, native to the Rocky

Mountains. The only lakes that had fish were where they could migrate upstream. Most of the hundreds of lakes in the Wind Rivers were in high glacial cirques with many steep waterfalls below that prevented fish from ever getting upstream.

The hatchery brought fish to us in five gallon milk cans, twelve cans at a time. We would put these twelve cans on six pack horses, a can on each side and pack them out into the mountains. In the seven years we were there, we packed out two and a half million little trout. They could be rainbow, cutthroat, California golden, brook, or German brown. We stocked 314 lakes during the time we ran our fishing camp, free for the public.

We put burlap on top of the cans so as the horses walked along the cans would splash and aerate the water but the fish couldn't splash out. We had to keep the horses moving. Even while loading up, someone had to lead the loaded ones around to keep the water splashing to get oxygen into it or else the fish would smother. Another problem with the burlap covers was that a lot of water would splash out. Every couple of miles the water would get too low so we'd stop at the streams and refill the cans with little buckets, then go on.

These waters were all virgin and were just full of water lice, leaches, fresh water shrimp, and that kind of stuff so those fish just gorged themselves. Some of the brook trout weighed three pounds the third year. Even the hatchery superintendent was amazed at the fast growth.

Most of the lakes are deep and only a few ever winter kill the fish. What keeps them from winter killing is water coming in and going out. This keeps oxygen in the water

A pack-train of trout heading for a new home

when the lake is frozen over. If there is no inlet or outlet to keep oxygen in the water, the ice freezes solid up to the banks all around the lake keeping out the air and the fish will die. Mirror Lake winter killed quite often but in the spring during high water fish migrate up the outlet stream and the lake would be restocked naturally.

No one else did any stocking of these lakes at that time because we were the only ones in these mountains. Today only the Game and Fish Department does the stocking.

We established the little fishing camp, Mitchells Fishing Camp, on Mud Lake near the Big Sandy Openings. We started out with a twelve by fourteen foot wall tent with three foot walls and no floor. That was for us to live in, cook in and sleep in. We had a bed

9

in one corner and cook stove in the opposite corner. What we did was borrow ten horses. I had lived here since 1906 and I knew everybody. These ranchers all had old horses that they had practically retired and quit using. They had old worn out saddles that they had replaced with new ones. We managed to borrow ten horses with six saddles and four pack saddles.

We charged a dollar and a half a day for horses. We kept the dollar and gave fifty cents to the people we borrowed the horses from. Believe it or not, that first summer we made three hundred dollars and fifteen cents. We also served meals in the tent for fifty cents a meal. You'd be surprised how many people would like to eat with us.

We would take the people fishing on the horses and be sure they caught their fish. Our guide service was for free. When we first went in there, we had fish in Boulter, Dads, Donald, Big Sandy and Black Joe Lakes, all cutthroats. We either went up to Dads Lake on the Highline Trail or Big Sandy Lake on the Big Sandy Trail. After we'd been there three years we began to catch the fish we had planted. The success of our business was fishing our own fish. We had trouble at first because really the only lakes that had good fishing were Dads, Black Joe and Big Sandy.

The first year we were there we rigged up a couple of five gallon coal oil cans with the tops cut out and put wooden lids in them. We went to Big Sandy Lake and caught fish on hooks and released them in these cans of water. You couldn't catch too many because they would begin to die on you if someone didn't shake them all the time to splash oxygen into the water. The first trip we caught seventeen cutthroats, all about nine

or ten inches long. We packed them on a
horse up to Rapid Lake, about a mile away,
and turned them loose. That was the first
stocking we did by ourselves. Nobody said
anything about it, we were on our own.
Nowadays it's illegal to do that.

We left those fish alone for two years.
The second summer one day when we didn't have
anything to do my dad and I went up there to
see if they lived. The first fish I caught
was a male, a buck we called them. He was a
monster. He looked like you had blowed him
up with a pump he was so fat. They didn't
have time to grow much in length but they got
fat. He probably weighed three and a half
pounds. My dad said I'd better turn him
loose because it was possible we had only
planted one buck. The rest might be all
does. So I turned him loose and went on
around a couple of hundred feet and caught
another buck and he weighed five and a half
pounds. We measured him and he was pretty
near as long in circumference as he was
length in body. As an advertisement for our
fishing camp we kept him and brought him to
town and put him in Mike Dankowski's Sporting
Goods window on display. This brought us a
lot of business.

My wife and I ran the fishing camp. My
dad came in with us for three or four years
after my mother died.

Later on we were trying to find fish to
plant that would get bigger than the kinds
supplied by the hatchery. Everybody seemed
to want big trout. We took these same two
cans that we'd done our first planting with
and went over the Continental Divide at
Hailey Pass down to Grave Lake. This was the
only lake in the area that had mackinaw trout
in it.

It took us all day to get over there from

11

camp and we stayed overnight. Next morning we wanted to catch some small mackinaw and all we could catch were big ones. We caught five fish, two of them weighed three and a half pounds each and the other three were about two pounders. We put the three smaller ones in one can and the two big ones in the other. They were bent all the time but they kept flopping around all the way back. We packed them back as fast as we could get those horses back over the pass to our side. We had selected a beautiful lake to put them in and named it Mays Lake as we had to name and record all the lakes we planted fish in. We turned them loose and they were glad to get out of those cans and take off into the deep water. That was in 1933 and to this day I have never caught a fish in that lake. Other people are catching them though, and the biggest I know of was caught by my foreman on the railroad and it weighed ten and a half pounds. They all came from those five and are there to this day, forty years later.

Throughout this century I've roamed this wilderness, communing with nature, observing other creatures along with myself, merely desiring to live and let live. Because of this aloneness, I've learned to love, not only those of my own kind, but all life within a wilderness; the birds, the beasts, the trees, the flowers, and the grasses of the land. Only in wilderness, it seems, is man's love so thoroughly and completely returned, so unselfishly shared.

Finis Mitchell

Emma Mitchell

"Queen of the Camp"

Everybody liked the queen, the epicure of elaborate foods, with birthday cakes made in a dutch oven a specialty throughout the entire mountain range.

She was the main spoke in the wheel because heavy activity in high mountains with clean air gave people ravenous appetites every day in every way.

Food and Equipment List for Mountain Hikes

Breakfast Snacks:

Foods mixed and sacked for breakfasts. An individual may mix or combine any of the following foods he may desire: (Mix equals approximately one cup per sack.) Grape Nuts 1/4 cup, or Gerber baby oats 1/4 cup, or Gerber baby rice 1/4 cup, or Kellogg's High Protein Concentrate 1/4 cup, added to:

Wheat germ (2 tablespoons per sack)
Powdered cream (3 tablespoons per sack)
Dry powdered milk, 1/4 cup
Two teaspoons sugar per sack

For bulk and chew, add to any mixture: Chopped dates, prunes, raisins or nuts. Mix with water in pan from scout kit.

Regular Daytime Foods:

Fruit cake, candy bars (your own choice), dried fruits, beef jerky, cheese (swiss keeps best), nuts (cashew has most food value), shredded cocoanut, dried beef, chicken and beef bullion cubes (drink with water if not cooked), loaf of raisin bread for each day out, green pea or mushroom powdered soup, salami (will keep only about four days), protein tablets, vitamin C tablets, malted milk tablets.

General:

Pain tablets. Matches. Zinc Oxide. Tooth paste. Band-aids. Hand soap. Extra socks. Leather gloves. Face towel. Sun glasses. Elastic bandage or binders. Plastic cover for yourself and pack. Sleepingbag and pack of course. Fishing tackle if going fishing (no fish in glacial regions). Good pocket knife. Flashlight. Never wear shoes with leather soles in mountains. They get as slick as greased glass. Camera and film if desired.

HIKING INFORMATION

It's apt to snow anytime in this high country. The summer of 1974 it snowed on us the 6th and the 8th of August and three times afterwards before the first of September. These are the conditions people have to expect because the Wind Rivers is a rugged range. These summer storms are of short duration, however. If you get several inches of snow, just hole up somewhere and don't panic because it will melt off in two or three hours after the storm passes, up to 11,000 feet. Above that, it won't melt off the peaks probably until the following day, but it will melt off. There's no use getting excited and trying to run out of the mountains because it's just a summer storm and to be expected.

Supposing you're up on Fremont Peak without crampons and ropes and it comes up a storm and snowed four or five inches. You'd break your neck trying to get down off there without some assistance. So, sit down-- don't get panicky. You're always supposed to have sandwiches, candy bars or concentrated foods. You should have those things in your pocket or pack. I have a list of these foods that I take with me that never need to be cooked. I never build a fire when I'm above timberline. When you're in a dangerous place and a storm comes up, you should always seek shelter and sit down. You can always find big rocks to get under. Quite often you can stay completely dry while waiting out a summer storm. You should always have some kind of protection that you pack with you when you go into these mountains. You just don't go bare handed, you go prepared. Usually you will have established a base camp near where you're hiking or climbing and you'll head for that when a storm approaches.

A few times I have been caught by a storm away from camp and had to stay overnight. I always carry a sheet of plastic in my pocket for this emergency. Nowadays there is what is called a space blanket that is even better. You can back up against the rocks in a sheltered place, sit on the plastic or blanket and wrap it around you. The heat from your own body will take care of you.

Water is never a problem in the Wind Rivers. I never pack water because you can find it anywhere. There's only one place that doesn't have water and that's on part of the Glacier Trail coming out of Dubois. There is a sign there that says "No water for ten and a half miles." Here is the only place you need to carry a canteen in the whole range.

Evening alone in the mountains. No one to talk to. No one speaking out. No reply to my thoughts. Only the comfort of a murmuring breeze in the trees, the goodnight chirp of the snowbird fading with the night. The glistening of the moon on a distant glacier, the faint music of waterfalls scurrying down from them, seeking green valleys in which to pause momentarily before racing on to join waters from other glaciers, from other continents, from other celestial wildernesses, seeking eternal rest within the briny seas.

Then darkness hovers about me. Only the sound of growing grasses, of blossoming flowers, of countless stars like a million jewels set in a sea of sereneness beckoning me into peaceful slumber, a dream of fulfillment, of content in a wilderness. Only God can give this to man.

Finis Mitchell

GREEN RIVER LAKES ENTRANCE

Trails: Highline, Granite Lake, Square Top
Mountain Route, New Fork, Lakeside, Porcupine,
Clear Creek, Slide Creek, Flat Top Mountain
Route, Mill Creek Route, Roaring Fork,
Elbow Creek Route

U.S.G.S. Maps   Green River Lakes, Downs
Mountain, Square Top Mountain, Gannett Peak

The Highline Trail goes up Green River to
Summit Lake and all points beyond.   Granite
Lake Trail leads up to Granite Lake. The
Square Top Mountain Route is not a trail but
will get you from Granite Lake to the top of
Square Top Mountain. The New Fork Trail ends
on Clark Creek above Green River and begins
back over in the New Fork Park Entrance. The
Lakeside Trail goes up the west side of lower
Green River Lake. Procupine Trail leads to
Twin and Shirley Lakes, up Porcupine Canyon
to join the New Fork Trail. Clear Creek
Trail leads to Clear Lake. The Slide Creek
Trail goes to Slide Lake, Flat Top Mountain,
Lost Eagle Peak, Elbow Lake, Golden Lake,
Baker Lake, and the Continental Divide.   The
Flat Top Mountain Route leads from Slide Lake
to the top of Flat Top Mountain. Mill Creek
Route goes to Faler, Crescent, and Bear
Lakes. The Roaring Fork Trail leads to Faler
and a route to Bear Lakes.

To get to the trailhead, you go 6 miles
west of Pinedale on U.S. 191 then turn right
on to the Green River Lakes road (Wyo. 352)
which is oiled. Go on past Cora and soon the
pavement stops. From here on a ways it is
being oiled, with over 20 miles oiled now.
This road continues on and ends at the Green
River Lakes.

There is a 21 unit modern campground here, a large parking area for backpackers, and a loading area for horses.

HIGHLINE TRAIL

The Highline Trail follows pretty close to timberline the entire length of the Wind River Range, a hundred miles or more. It starts down near South Pass City and Atlantic City on the east and runs along the west side of the Continental Divide clear to Union Pass near Dubois. The part of the trail heavily used now is from the Green River Lakes to the Big Sandy Openings. The trail on either end is little used because of roads built into the area.

The Highline Trail goes up the northeast side of the Green River Lakes. There is a

Square Top Mtn. over Upper Green River Lake

trail on each side but the best one is the
newest one (Highline Trail) which crosses the
bridge at the outlet of the lake and goes
along the lake near the shoreline.

Right after you cross the bridge, less
than 100 yards, you cross Mill Creek. Walk
across a little flat in 18-inch willows and,
coming to a little bench, you climb up
probably eight or ten feet into the
sagebrush. Right there the trail forks. The
upper left hand trail is the old trail that
leads up into Clear Creek Basin.

The main trail (Highline Trail) follows
right along the lake shore for about 2 1/2
miles and comes to a foot bridge on Clear
Creek on the lake level below Clear Creek
Falls. About a half mile further brings you
near the bridge crossing the river where the
trail coming up the other side of the lake
(Lakeside Trail) joins the Highline Trail.

The Highline Trail leads 1/2 mile to the
upper lake. Follow trail to its upper end,
then go on up Green River. Straight ahead of
you now looms Square Top Mountain. There are
nice camping spots in the trees along the
river. The river is slightly murky from
glacial dust and there are no fish, but it's
good drinking water. Towering above you on
the left along here is White Rock Mountain,
11,284 feet.

The trail follows the river right on up
the valley, crossing Elbow and Pixley Creeks
and the first bridge you come to crossing
Green River is at the upper end of Beaver
Park.

White Rock Mtn. over Upper Green River Lake

ELBOW CREEK ROUTE

To go to Elbow Lake and the Golden Lakes follow the Highline Trail up the Green River to Elbow Creek. Follow up on the left side of Elbow Creek (no trail) for about a mile. It is quite steep through here. When you get to where there is a bare hillside across the creek from you, cross the stream and zig-zag up that bare hillside. Eventually, before you get into the sheer ledges, you work into and cross the creek again just below a junction where another stream comes in from the east. There is a faint trail now going on up Elbow Creek on the left side to Elbow Lake and a route on up the stream to Golden Lakes.

Horses can get into these lakes by coming up another way, the Slide Creek Route described elsewhere.

GRANITE LAKE TRAIL

A short distance after crossing the bridge a faint trail takes off to the right with a sign showing the Granite Lake Trail. This trail, an old horse trail, is very difficult to follow unless you've had a lot of mountain experience. In 1953 there was a big forest fire here. It burnt the whole side of the mountain and it's still the mess that it was when the fire went out.

SQUARETOP MOUNTAIN ROUTE

If you want to climb Square Top, after you cross the foot bridge on the Green River you go about 150 feet out into the woods and you come into the upper end of a big park. You go over to the edge of the timber and follow it down until you get down to and beyond the forest fire and downed timber. Then there is a draw comes right down from Granite Lake to the river, with green live timber in it. You work your way up the draw, past the burned area and pick up the old horse trail and go on to the lake. The route on up to Square Top is not difficult. The smallest child I ever took up there was four years old, but you have to hand him up over the ledges in a lot of places.

You go right around the right hand side of the lake to the outlet and cross (no trouble crossing). You go back around the lake part way and take up a little tiny stream that comes off of Square Top. You follow that stream clear up till you get above timberline, crossing a lot of snow. There's a break in the ledges and you can go clear to the top. When you get out on top,

then in order to look back down to Green
River Lakes (you're on the rear end of the
top) you have to go about a mile and a half
over the top to where you can look back down
over the lakes. From the main trail it's a
couple of miles to Granite Lake, then about
another mile to the top. On top you don't
have to go clear to the front to get a good
view. You can stay along the right side and
go out on points where you can see the river
and your trail all the way up. You can turn
around when you get on top and see clear back
to Gannet Peak and a lot of the glaciers.
You're at 11,695 feet, about three and a half
thousand feet above the river.

Most younger groups such as Boy or Girl
Scouts take two days going from the end of
the road to the bridge at Beaver Park. There
are numerous camping spots all over the area.
From the bridge to the top of Square Top and
back is a good day's hike for this age group
and families.

Going on up the Green River, it is all
easy hiking along here. Tourist, Wells, and
Trail Creeks join the Green River along here
under two thousand foot cliffs above on the
left. There are no trails or routes going up
Tourist, Wells, or Green River at this point.

The Highline Trail leaves the river here
and switchbacks up the west slope beside
Trail Creek, finally crossing the stream as
you come out on top. A short distance
further near the junction of Clark and Trail
Creeks, a sign gives these directions: along
the New Fork Trail which goes up Clark Creek
it's 7 miles to the Porcupine Trail, 9 miles
to New Fork Park, 17 miles to New Fork Lake;
along the Highline Trail up Trail Creek it's 3
miles to Summit Lake, 18 miles to Elkheart
Park, or 12 miles back to Green River Lakes.

Following the Highline Trail you climb

22

gradually up the creek until you reach Green River Pass at 10,362 foot elevation. Then you descend a little to Summit Lake, at 10,324 ft.

The Green River has its beginning in the glaciers up against the Continental Divide between Gannet Peak and Bow Mountain. The largest of these is Mammoth Glacier covering several square miles west of the divide. An old trail to these glaciers takes off from the Highline Trail about two miles below Green River Pass and about a mile above Trail Creek Park where Clark Creek comes in. This trail climbs steeply up above a stream about a mile to Vista Pass then stays fairly level as it swings around the mountain to the Green River. From here, rock slides have closed the trail to horses but hikers can make their way up the river to Dale Lake. Above Dale Lake the route goes through Cube Rock Pass over to Peak Lake. Another trail coming from Shannon Pass called the Shannon Pass Trail runs south about two miles to join the Highline Trail.

To get to Mammoth Glacier from Peak Lake, first cross outlet below lake or below Little Peak Lake if water is high, then go around the north side of the lake to the east end and follow up the stream past some small long lakes to the upper end of the last long lake, then swing off to the left. You climb up the mountain, going through the saddle left of Split Mountain, then down onto Mammoth Glacier.

Ladd Peak gives an excellent view across the glaciers to Gannet Peak. It can be reached by going north from Peak Lake down to Stonehammer Lake, about a mile away. From about halfway along the east side of the lake, you climb up a draw between the ledges then head north again aiming for the west end

23

of the peak. When you reach the high ground, it levels off and you go east right on up to the top.

Titcomb Canyon can also be reached from Peak Lake, from where you can go on up to Gannet Peak. Going east up the creek entering Peak Lake, you pass a series of long slender lakes and continue right on up the stream staying on its left side all the way (no trail). In the upper end of the canyon you climb almost straight east, aiming for the pass between Twin Peaks and Winifred Peak. You pass through onto Knapsack Col on the upper end of Twins Glacier. Stay high as you can as you continue due east where in about a mile and a half you'll join the Titcomb Canyon Trail going up to Dinwoody Pass. This is one of the two main trails to Gannett Peak and is described in another part of this book.

NEW FORK TRAIL

Back at Clark Creek, the New Fork Trail takes off to the west and climbs steeply for about a mile and a half up to Clark Lake. There are several nice campsites as you reach the lake. It's a very scenic place, with cliffs, ledges and peaks, surrounding you in all directions. The trail climbs out on the far end of the small valley to a saddle at about 11,000 feet. This will be your highest point along this trail. Continuing on you'll go down some, then climb again to Lozier Lakes. This is all above timberline in true alpine country. Fishing is good at the upper Lozier Lake and camping is among the rocks as there are no trees around this lake.

Kenny Lake above Lozier Lakes can be

reached by going cross country from about half way between Lozier Lakes and the saddle above Clark Lake. There is no trail but the country is open and you can easily make your way the mile or so to Kenny Lake. Also from along this same high ground you can go south cross country to Thompson Lakes and Glover Peak. More directions on this will be given in another section of this guide.

Leaving Lozier Lakes going west, the trail approaches the edge of a canyon, then descends steeply over many switchbacks to join the Porcupine Trail. At this trail junction a sign doesn't mention Porcupine Trail or Dodge Creek. You just turn right (north) to go up the Porcupine Trail and just around the corner you'll cross Dodge Creek where there's a nice grassy place to camp. If you left your car at Green River Lakes and want to make a loop trail, continue up Porcupine Trail and it will take you back to Green River Lakes, coming in on the south side between the upper and lower lakes. From here it's two miles back to your car along the southwest side of the lake. If you continue down on the New Fork Trail you'll reach New Fork Park and New Fork River in about a mile.

LAKESIDE TRAIL

From the upper end of the campground at Green River Lakes a trail begins and goes along the west side of the lower lake. On this one you can cross over between the lakes and join the Highline Trail on Green River or turn right up Porcupine Creek and go up the Porcupine Trail.

At the beginning you'll climb up and down steps to get across a fence, then continue right along the lake. When you get up to the park, there's a signboard there and you can either go over, cross the bridge and join the Highline Trail, or turn right on the Porcupine Trail.

PORCUPINE TRAIL

This trail begins near the end of the Lakeside Trail at the upper end of Lower Green Lake. You start climbing in the timber and soon get to Porcupine Falls on the right.

It's about two miles of climbing to get out of the canyon. As you level off, there's a sign there pointing out a trail branching off that goes up to Twin, Shirley, and Valaite Lakes. A horse trail continues between Twin Lakes and ends at Shirley Lake. There are fish in all these lakes. These lakes are just above the timber in the open. You can follow up the drainage above Shirley to get to Valaite Lake. You can camp anywhere along here. These lakes and Slide Lake are probably the closest small fishing lakes near the Green River Lakes.

Porcupine Trail continues on up the valley with high cliffs and ridges on each side until it reaches the end of the valley. Here the Jim Creek Trail enters from the canyon on the right and the main trail climbs gradually, then switchbacks steeply to Porcupine Pass. From here you have a grand view down Porcupine Canyon on one side and New Fork Canyon on the other. The trail zigzags down the other side and joins the New Fork Trail about a mile above New Fork Park.

CLEAR CREEK TRAIL

This trail begins after crossing the bridge at the outlet of Lower Green Lake.

Right after you get off the bridge, about 150 feet, you come to Mill Creek and when you cross it there's a signboard there where the trail forks. The upper left hand trail is the old trail that leads up into Clear Creek Basin. You follow this trail along the mountainside and in about four miles you reach a natural bridge at far end of Clear Creek Basin. The trail ends about a mile below Clear Lake in a little park. From where the trail ends it's not too difficult to hike on in to this lake, except for very small children. You follow the stream on up and eventually you'll reach the outlet of Clear Lake.

It's a very scenic area. The ledges rise 2,700 feet on north side of Clear Lake and 2,495 feet on the other. There is forest on the north side only. There are no fish in Clear Lake.

SLIDE CREEK TRAIL

This trail begins part way up Clear Creek (see Clear Creek Trail for the beginning). The trail branches off to the south and crosses Clear Creek on a footbridge at signboards several hundred yards below where Slide Creek enters. You walk up across the meadow and cross Slide Creek as you enter the trees (no footbridge). Immediately you zig-zag sharply up the mountain. About a mile from Clear Creek you reach Slide Creek Falls. Above the falls the trail starts to level out somewhat for about a mile along a big meadow to Fish Bowl Springs which is in timber. Here you climb steeply again and shortly reach the outlet of the lake.

SLIDE CREEK ROUTE

Start out on the Slide Creek Trail as if you were going to Slide Lake. After climbing all the switchbacks and passing Slide Creek Falls you'll come to a big open meadow. At the upper side of the meadow you leave the main trail and go off to the right around the edge of the timber. You don't go into the trees, you go around them to the stream and find a way to cross it - you may have to wade. From here you follow a slight trail up an opening in the timber climbing steadily to the left. You'll enter the trees and then come to a stream coming down from the basin above to the south. After crossing this stream you'll find a horse trail that follows on up the stream and then on up the bottom of the canyon behind White Rock. You'll break out into some open meadows and then leave the timber entirely. You zig-zag through the rocks on up the canyon to the head of it and then turn left into a pass.

From the pass you go down into a big saddle from where you can look down into Slide Lake. From there you climb east up a narrow ridge clear on up to a big plateau which is Lost Eagle Peak at its high point (bottle on summit). If you want to turn left and go back towards the north side, you come to the cliffs and can see for miles across the country and take pictures into Slide Creek Gorge.

To get to Elbow Lake No. 2 you go east as far as you can to the edge of the cliffs and then turn right. There is no trail on this plateau but when you start south along the east side, a trail forms because this is the only route down to the lake. You go south and down enough to get below the cliffs and

then swing back down to the left to the lake.
(Elbow Lake #2.)

Going on from Elbow Lake No. 2, you go
east up out of the basin and then go south
down to Elbow Lake #1. From here you go on
to the Golden Lakes, upstream.

From the first Golden Lake a route takes
off north and east to Baker Lake (of course
no trail). You work your way north and then
swing gradually east up a mountain into the
upper headwaters of Slide Creek. You pass
through a saddle west of Baker Lake and
descend to the lake itself.

From the upper end of the Golden Lakes a
route takes off from the north end going east
and then northeast across to the same saddle
west of Baker Lake.

Baker Lake lies right against the
Continental Divide. To reach the divide you
can go around either side but the south side
is best. From the saddle west of the lake
you don't go right down to the lake, you stay
about on the same level and work your way
around the lake and then go down to cross
Pixley Creek where it leaves the lake.
Climbing again up the ridge to the east and
to the right from the outlet you continue
around the lake and cross the glacial moraine
between Baker and Iceberg Lake and climb a
ways up to the saddle where you're on the
Continental Divide.

FLAT TOP MOUNTAIN ROUTE

Lots of people like to get on top of Flat
Top Mountain because of the spectacular view
from there. You go to the outlet of Slide
Lake where the trail ends. Then you can go
around the left hand side of the lake -
there's no trail but it's not bad walking.
Stay on the left side of Slide Creek above

the lake, follow it up to the first stream that comes in from your left. Cross this creek, then you can work your way up the stream, into a basin that has two or three little lakes in it. Climb up out of this basin, going north, swing around to the west and you're on a big, fairly flat open mesa. Mountain sheep live up here year around. It's so flat that the wind keeps the snow blown off so they can live there. Going west you go through Ram Pass which is a narrow place between the steep cliffs on both sides. From here you can follow the sheep trails all around the rim and even out on a long ridge to the north of the summit.

From back where you got on the summit, you can go north from there, out along a ridge, clear out to a point just above Clear Lake. There is no way down from the mesa except back the way you came.

MILL CREEK ROUTE

Another way to get to Faler Lake and Bear Lake which is a very, very attractive and scenic route and anyone can walk it is to go up Mill Creek. This trail takes off less than half a mile north of the bridge crossing the outlet of Lower Green Lake, on the north side. Follow the main trail 1/2 mile along a fence and turn right up a ridge which bears right up Mill Creek.

The trail goes about two-thirds of the way up the creek 2-1/2 to 3 miles, crosses Mill Creek, then turns off from the creek and goes up south in timber around the ledges and up into a pass. Go left from the pass and within 400 feet you're above timberline where the trail disappears because it's never used. You can just walk on up over this whole open mountain, clear around the summit to the east end. You can't go anywhere but the right place because you're surrounded by thousand foot ledges. You're up on a big, flat mesa, looking down at everything. You go east as far as you can go, out on a point where you can descend along a ridge to join the horse trail to Faler Lake.

You couldn't get a horse off the mesa on this route but experienced hikers would have little problem.

From where you join the horse trail, the best way to Bear Lake is past Crescent Lake. Instead of following the horse trail, you cross it and climb the other side and you'll reach the outlet of Crescent Lake in about a half mile. This lake has steep ledges on the south side and gentle slopes along the north and contains cutthroat trout. Follow around the north side, cross the stream just above where it enters the lake and start climbing. The route follows a general southerly direction in the high country to Bear Lake.

This is all high mountain sheep country and you just might see some elk.

ROARING FORK ROUTE

At the bridge crossing the river at the outlet of Lower Green River Lake, you take the left fork of the trail after crossing the bridge and follow the fence and go over along the horsetrail to Roaring Fork. Follow this trail up past Native Lake (has cutthroat trout) and on to where it ends at Faler Lake which has Golden Trout in it. This is about twelve miles from where you started at Green River Lakes.

Bear Lake can be reached from Faler Lake by following up a stream that comes in from the north into the northeast corner of the

lake. Climb up this stream until you top out
and you'll be in the mountain sheep country,
all above timberline. Then staying above the
ledges you can work your way south to Bear
Lake about three miles cross-country.

You should plan on three or four days at
least for this trip. A week is better to get
acquainted with the country and have a lot of
fun exploring.

NEW FORK LAKES ENTRANCE

Trails: New Fork Canyon, Palmer Lake,
         Glover Peak Route

U.S.G.S. Maps: New Fork Lakes, Kendall
Mountain, Square Top Mountain, Double Top
Mountain

New Fork Trail goes up New Fork Canyon to
Lozier Lakes, Clark Lake, and joins Highline
Trail at Trail Creek Park. Palmer Lake Trail
goes up Palmer Canyon to Palmer Lake, Round
Lake and Section Corner Lake.

On the Green River Lakes road there is a
sign showing the road to New Fork Lakes with
mileages two and a half miles to the lake,
and three and a half miles to the campground
at the Narrows between the two lakes where
the road ends. There's an old dam at the
outlet of the lake but you turn off to the
left before you get to it and go on up the
north side of the lake to the Narrows
Campground. There are camping places with
tables and water and a parking area for cars.
There's also a loading place for horses here.
These lakes set in the timber except for the

north side which has patches of sagebrush.
The campground is in the timber.

Hikers using this entrance are generally
heading for the high country around Lozier
Lakes or up Palmer Canyon to Palmer Lake.
You can come on around Doubletop Mountain
from Palmer Lake, back past Rainbow Lake on
the Doubletop Mountain Trail, then cross back
to New Fork Lakes to complete the loop at
your car.

NEW FORK CANYON TRAIL

The New Fork Canyon Trail starts at the
Narrows Campground and follows above the lake
to the upper end of the valley where it goes
up New Fork River. There is a trail junction
as you reach the river where the right branch
goes back to join the Doubletop Mountain
Trail, returning to its beginning at the
Willow Creek Guard Station.

The main trail goes on up New Fork River,
climbing gradually all the way. It is a very
scenic trail with cliffs, ledges and rock
slides all the way. You can camp anywhere
along the river and return, or go as far as
you want--clear to the Green River Lakes, or
over to Summit Lake and return past Palmer
Lake.

You'll climb some before getting to New
Fork Park, where at the upper end the Palmer
Lake Trail takes off to the right. The main
trail leaves the river and climbs a ridge
where in about a mile the Porcupine Trail
joins from the left and runs up to Porcupine
Pass and on over to Green River Lakes.

The New Fork Trail continues climbing on
up the ridge high above the river then zig-
zags steeply up a side canyon for about a
mile to the top. From there, you're just a
short distance to Lozier Lake. This is a

34

Nice catch from Cutthroat and No Name Lakes

nice fishing lake, sitting in high alpine country above timberline. You can find campsites among the rocks on the east side of the lake.

The trail descends to the lower Lozier Lake which is a small lake of little interest, then begins to climb again towards the pass above Clark Lake. About half way to the pass, you can go cross-country to the north about a mile to Kenny Lake, much larger than upper Lozier and a nice place to fish and explore around. There are no trails leading to it, but the country is open in all directions and you're on top of the country.

From this high country trail you can also take off cross country to the south to Thompson and Hidden Lakes (all have brook trout 1974), and up to Glover Peak. From any of these places you can make your way on south to join the Doubletop Mountain Trail. Better descriptions of these cross-country routes are given in another section of this guide.

GLOVER PEAK ROUTE

Starting between the two No Name Lakes on Doubletop Mountain Trail you head pretty much straight north, avoiding the ledges and going around the little lakes. In about a mile and a half you'll reach the main lake that's quite glaciated and sits on the west side of Glover Peak. Follow up the stream coming into this lake and cross it about half way up. At the top, it comes out at a nice big lake but I don't think there are any fish in it. You turn to the right and without too much trouble you can follow the ridge all the way to the summit of the north portion of the peak. From between the two points you overlook a glacier on the east slope. You can see clear to the Continental Divide from here, including Gannett Peak and all the glaciers below it. The south peak is the highest but you can't reach it from the west side without ropes and climbing gear.

You can reach Glover Peak from the New Fork Trail also. Starting at the pass above Clark Lake you turn south staying high and head for the only high peak in sight to the southeast. All the rest are just rolling glacial hills and lakes. The highest summit is easiest from south, NW of Summit Lake on Highline Trail.

Route to Thompson Lakes and Hidden Lakes

This is not a trail but there have been horses through there so it is not a difficult route. You go around the east end of Upper No Name Lake and head northwest through a little saddle. Continue north about a half

NEW FORK LAKES, WILLOW CREEK AND SPRING CREEK ENTRANCES

37

mile and go between two little lakes on the
stream that comes down from Glover Peak.
Then head northwest for about a mile till you
reach the first of Thompson Lakes. This is
all above timberline so is open enough so you
can see all over the place. You can make
your way on foot around to both Thompson
Lakes and Hidden Lakes (all brook trout
1974). But, if you're going on over to the
New Fork Trail to the north, go north from
the east side of Big Thompson Lake up onto
the plateau above. Heading north from here
you bear off to the right enough to get
around the big ledges that build up before
you reach the trail. Once around the ledges
you descend into the valley and the trail is
part way up the other side. Lozier Lakes
will be about a mile west and Clark Lake
about two miles east. Both are good places
to camp and have good fishing for small
trout.

From the pass on the New Fork Trail,
you'll descend on switchbacks for about a
mile to Clark Lake which sits in the bottom
of an alpine valley, surrounded by cliffs,
peaks and ledges. There are nice campsites
in the trees in the upper end of the valley
(packers have their horse camp here), or
there are several good hiking campsites
around the lower end of the lake. From here
the trail descends steeply for about a mile
and a half and ends where it joins the
Highline Trail on Trail Creek. From here you
can go right on up to Summit Lake and back
around to Palmer Lake and return down Palmer
Canyon to rejoin the New Fork Trail, or go
left down the Green River and come out at the
Green River Lakes Campground.

PALMER LAKE TRAIL

You can turn up Palmer Canyon on your way up New Fork River if you want to get a lot of fishing. This is the Palmer Lake Trail and follows up Reynolds Creek about three miles to Palmer Lake. This lake is fished pretty heavily by the people from the dude ranches.

For real good fishing, go on over to Cutthroat and No Name Lakes. The main trail over there crosses Lake Creek 1 mile north of the inlet of Palmer Lake and goes east about two miles to Cutthroat Lakes. Another route takes off cross-country at the outlet of Palmer Lake, leaving the Palmer Lake Trail going almost straight east about a mile and a half to Cutthroat Lakes. This is a much better trail than the Doubletop Mountain Trail running from Palmer to Cutthroat Lakes. There is no sign where the short-cut trail takes off but there are signs on the Doubletop Mountain Trail at the outlet of Palmer Lake, one distance given is Summit Lake 6 miles.

From Cutthroat Lakes you climb into another drainage to No Name Lakes. From there the trail goes on down and eventually gets to Summit Lake. A lot of the dude outfits camp and fish at Summit Lake, so hikers may want to camp somewhere else.

Today we met, deep within a wilderness. And today we will part, each going his own way, perhaps never to meet again in this lifetime. But a friendship has been formed, a love developed, a knowledge received that man can live in peace and quiet in a world of turmoil.

Finis Mitchell

Two limits of cutthroats

WILLOW CREEK ENTRANCE

Trails: Section Corner Lake, Doubletop
Mountain

U.S.G.S. Maps: New Fork Lakes, Fremont Lake
North

Doubletop Mountain Trail goes to Palmer
Lake, Cutthroat Lakes, No Name Lakes and on
to Summit Lake. Section Corner Lake Trail
goes to Section Corner Lake and on to Trapper
Lake.

This trail starts near the Willow Creek
Guard Station. To get there, turn north from
U.S. 187 about six miles west of Pinedale
onto the Green River Lakes road. Go about

three miles north of Cora and turn right. A sign here points to Willow Creek Guard Station. Section Corner Lake Trail and Doubletop Mountain Trail start about a half mile beyond the station.

DOUBLETOP MOUNTAIN TRAIL

The Doubletop Mountain Trail takes off to the left and is part of the Lowline Trail for about two miles. You'll climb about a thousand feet up out of the canyon before you'll reach a fork in the trail. The Lowline Trail takes off to the left and drops about a thousand feet to the New Fork River Trail where you could go back to the Narrows Campground.

Turning right at the above fork in the Lowline trail and you're on Doubletop Mountain Trail which leads past Doubletop Mountain and Palmer Lake and continues to its end at Summit Lake where it joins the Highline Trail.

About six miles from the trail's beginning at the guard station will bring you to Rainbow Lake which is about, 2,000 feet higher than where you started. It's a steady climb all the way but a pretty one, with small streams and occassional marshes along the trail. There's good fishing at this lake. Above the lake the trail breaks out above timberline and begins to level out a bit as you near the summit of Doubletop Mountain. A trail running south to join the Section Corner Lake Trail joins here. Your trail skirts the south side of Doubletop about 700 feet below the summit then descends to cross the Palmer Lake Trail above the entrance to Palmer Lake.

Continuing east on Doubletop Trail in about 2 miles past Palmer Lake you'll reach

Cutthroat Lakes, then soon you'll come to No Name Lakes. These all have excellent fishing. From the farthest of these lakes you'll descend to Summit Lake to join the Highline Trail. This lake is fished quite heavily by packer groups that camp around it.

From Summit Lake you could loop down the Pine Creek Canyon Trail to Trapper Lake, over to Section Corner Lake, then west to your car at Willow Creek Guard Station. In a long meadowed park, where the trail crosses a heavily-used horse trail, a sign says Section Corner Lake 2 miles. This south trail ends at Lozier Ranch.

SECTION CORNER LAKE TRAIL

Section Corner Lake Trail branches to the right shortly after the trails beginning near the guard station. It climbs steadily for over two miles, up over a thousand feet to near the top of a long ridge where a secondary trail branches to the left and runs up the ridge, over the summit and on north through high country to join the Doubletop Mountain Trail close to the summit of the mountain.

Continuing east on Section Corner Lake Trail you'll round the ridge and go through some beautiful, scenic high country to Section Corner Lake. This is a large lake with plenty of places to camp around it.

Near the Lake Creek outlet from the lake, a trail runs almost straight north to Round and Palmer Lakes. It's about 2 1/2 miles to Round and another mile and a half to Palmer. Just after passing Round Lake, the Heart Lake Trail takes off to the right to Dean Lake, about a mile away. From Dean it's about a mile and a half down to Heart Lake. There are nice two to three pound Rainbows here.

Just above Heart Lake, the trail branches. One trail goes around the east side and over to shortly join the Pine Creek Canyon Trail at Gottfried Lake. The other trail goes around the west side and down about a mile, passing some small lakes, to Trail Lake and joins the Pine Creek Canyon Trail beyond it. Near the east side of Trail Lake a trail takes off and goes over to Neil Lake. This one goes on up to rejoin the Pine Creek Canyon Trail at Gottfried Lake. All these lakes have cutthroat trout in them except for Heart Lake, which has rainbows. This is all high scenic forest country.

From Gottfried Lake the Pine Creek Canyon Trail goes on to Borum Lake, about a mile away. You go right along the shoreline of Borum (which has cutthroat trout in it also) then on about two miles to Summit Lake where you'll join the Highline Trail.

From Section Corner Lake the trail continues east, climbing up and over into the next drainage to descend a little to Trapper Lake, about a mile away.

At Trapper Lake, trails lead north to Palmer and Summit Lakes, and south to Spring Creek Park, Upper Fremont Lake Campground, and Elkhart Guard Station, which is a main entrance.

We must strive to preserve this wilderness for innocent souls yet to follow in our footsteps; that they too, may enjoy a wilderness with all its bounties, and learn to preserve it for those to follow them.

Finis Mitchell

SPRING CREEK PARK ENTRANCE

Trails: Glimpse Lake, Trapper Lake

U.S.G.S. Map: Fremont Lake South

Glimpse Lake Trail is a new easy trail to Glimpse Lake and joins Pine Creek Trail on the ridge just above Glimpse Lake. Trapper Lake Trail is a higher trail going to Trapper Lake and joins the Pine Creek Trail and Section Corner Trail. Pine Creek Trail will take you on to Summit Lake.

To get to Spring Creek Park, take U.S. 191, turn off on second street to right, west of Pine Creek bridge in town of Pinedale. This is the Willow Lake road. You'll come first to Soda Lake which has brook trout and German browns in it. There is also an elk feeding grounds here. You continue on the Willow Lake road to just before you get to a dugway (that goes up over a hill and down to Willow Lake). When you cross a cattle guard in a fence, there's a road that turns to the right that goes on up to Spring Creek Park. This is a rough road and recommended for jeeps and pickup trucks. If you are a good mountain road driver, with care you can negotiate the rocks and ruts in a sedan most of the way. Plans are to improve this road for sedan use so inquire in Pinedale if you plan to use it.

GLIMPSE LAKE TRAIL

The Glimpse Lake Trail beginning here is a good new trail. It's about five miles to Glimpse Lake where you can catch nice brook trout. The trail goes around the south side of the lake crossing the outlet and joins the Pine Creek Canyon Trail on the east side on top of a timbered ridge. This trail going south drops about 2,000 feet to where it branches at Pine Creek. The right branch goes down to Upper Fremont Lake Campground which is a secondary entrance reachable only by boat or foot trails. The left branch goes up Fremont Creek about a mile to Long Lake where it forks. The right fork goes down to the Upper Fremont Lake Campground. The left branch crosses over into the Faler Creek Drainage and continues up above the stream to Elkhart Park which is a main entrance.

The Glimpse Lake Trail is a much better route to Glimpse Lake and places north of there than coming from Elkhart Park. From the latter, you hike about the same distance but you descend 2,000 feet, then climb up 2,000 feet to get to Glimpse Lake. From Spring Creek Park you gradually climb about one thousand feet to the lake.

From Glimpse Lake you can follow on up the Pine Creek Canyon Trail past Prospector Lake (off the trail), Little Trapper Lake, then on to Trapper Lake where this trail goes on north to Summit Lake. The Section Corner Lake Trail comes in at Trapper Lake going west. Either one of these trails has branches that will take you to the Palmer Lake area also.

TRAPPER LAKE TRAIL

The Trapper Lake Trail starting at Spring Creek Park is a jeep road and an old stock trail going to Trapper Lake. The wilderness boundary prevents jeeps from going very far on this road. This trail pretty much parallels the Glimpse Lake Trail but is from a half mile to a little over a mile west of it. In about 3 1/2 miles it crosses over to Trapper Creek and follows it about another three miles on to Trapper Lake. It joins the Section Corner Lake Trail below Trapper Lake about a quarter mile down stream.

Also from Spring Creek Park the Willow Lake Trail takes off to the northwest, descends past the northeast tip of Willow Lake and continues across the meadow to Lake Creek. After crossing this creek, it joins the Snake Lake Trail, going up Lake Creek a little over a mile to Snake Lake where it ends. (This used to be Section Corner Lake Trail from Lozier Box R Ranch.)

ELKHART PARK ENTRANCE

Trails: Pine Creek Canyon, Pole Creek, Gannett Peak from Dinwoody Pass Route, Indian Pass Trail, Glacier Trail, Titcomb Lakes

U.S.G.S. Maps: Fremont Lake North, Bridger Lakes

Pole Creek Trail is the beginning of a route to Island Lake, Titcomb Basin and Gannett Peak. You begin on Pole Creek Trail, then Seneca Lake Trail, Indian Pass Trail and Titcomb Basin Trail. Triple signboard near Ecklund Lake. Highline Trail is reached at the end of the Pole Creek Trail at Pole Creek Lakes and runs to Cook Lakes, Little Seneca Lake, Jean Lakes, Elbow Lake and on to Summit Lake and beyond. Pine Creek Canyon Trail goes to Long Lake, Glimpse Lake, Trapper Lake, Gottfried and Borum Lakes and ends at Summit Lake on the Highline Trail.

Two main trails begin here, the Pine Creek Canyon Trail and the Pole Creek Trail. A paved road starting east out of Pinedale going to Fremont Lake runs all the way to the Trails End Campground where the trails begin. The campground is clean and well developed and has a parking area that can handle over fifty cars. There are unloading facilities for horses also.

The main use of Elkhart Park for hikers is to reach Island Lake and Fremont Peak and the Cook Lake area. These places are reached by using the Pole Creek Trail which is one of the heaviest used trails on the west slope. It's a very good trail and well signed.

POLE CREEK TRAIL

The Pole Creek Trail begins on the east side of the road between the campground and the Ranger Station, right out of the parking lot and horse chute. It goes up Faler Creek about a mile and a half to the end of the creek then on up over a saddle. Here it levels off, swinging around to the northeast and enters the Wilderness Area. Passing the east end of Miller Park you reach a sign pointing to Miller Lake, about a half mile below. People hike over from Elkhart Park to fish for brook trout here and come back the same day. The trail goes around the south side of the lake and on over to Middle Sweeney Lake which has good cutthroat fishing. This trail goes up to Upper Sweeney, then on to join the Pole Creek Trail. The Sweeney Lakes Trail is a pack trail coming up from Half Moon Lake and is a much longer and rougher route to Sweeney Lakes than the main one coming from Elkhart Park.

Back at Miller Park you climb gradually through an open big meadow mostly full of short willows where you are quite apt to see moose, especially in the morning and evening. The trail goes into the timber, then through another opening and eventually goes out on Photographers Point. There's a rock by the trail here at a tiny lake where people sit to take pictures. A much better view is available down and out on the point itself.

Leaving Photographers Point you go through quite a bit of timber and come to a sign pointing to Sweeney Lake, one mile.

About a half mile further through timber the Seneca Lake Trail comes in between Barbara and Eklund Lakes. There's a triangular shaped sign board at this junction giving directions. To the left you go up to Island Lake. To the right are Pole Creek and Cook Lakes.

Continuing on the Pole Creek Trail, you go around the south end of Eklund Lake, up a little dugway and it's about three miles to lower Pole Creek crossing. There are no fish along this stretch of the trail which has no major climbs except for a little coming up at the beginning and going down at the end. In the trees just after the creek crossing there are several large camping places. The long, deep bay along here has excellent fishing. It's one of the arms of Pole Creek Lakes. Here Pole Creek Trail ends as it joins the Highline Trail which comes up from the Chain Lakes below and goes on past the Cook Lakes above. Going upstream, the signboards are in the trees there and you go up to the left and around the head of a little lake and cross the main stream. You continue on about two miles where the Fremont Trail comes in from the right, about a half mile short of Cook Lakes.

Back at Eklund Lake where the big triangular sign is, if you go to the left (north) you'll be on the Seneca Lake Trail which goes toward the Island Lake country. You proceed around Barbara Lake, down the creek a ways, and up to Hobbs Lake.

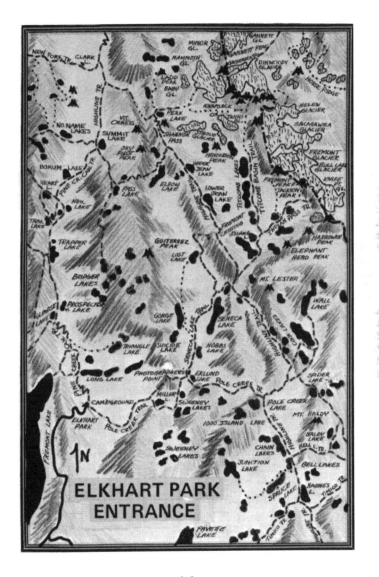

ELKHART PARK
ENTRANCE

Gorge Lake can be reached by following down the stream at the outlet of Hobbs Lake. There is a bridge crossing the stream at the Hobbs Lake outlet. You stay on the west side of the stream and make your way down across the rock slides to Gorge Lake. There is good fishing there.

Then if you want to go on down to Suicide Lake, you go to the left to the outlet of Gorge Lake. (The best fishing is in this long neck of the lake.) You can't cross the stream so you stay on the left side and make your way about a half mile down to the inlet of Suicide Lake. You have to do quite a bit of climbing and winding around to get there. It's good fishing here. You can work your way around the south side of the lake to near the outlet, but it's not easy. That's why I named this lake "Suicide Lake." If you want to commit suicide, it's pretty easy to do it here. On the other side, the ledges run sheer into the water.

Back at Hobbs Lake, the Seneca Lake Trail (which is also the Island Lake Trail) crosses the footbridge at the outlet and continues, where in about a half mile you'll cross the stream below Seneca Lake.

At the stream crossing you may have trouble crossing on foot during high water. In that case go upstream a ways where you'll find places to cross on the rocks then come back to the trail. You go on through a flat area east of a tiny lake then you go down, and I mean down, till you get into another basin. Then you have to climb right back up again, up till you come out on top where you can look out on Seneca Lake. The trail goes all along the left shore where during high water you have to climb the ledges in places because the water gets over two feet deep over the trail. In the summer of 1974, the

Forest Service promised me they would send someone up there to build this trail high enough to get above the water.

After you leave Seneca Lake, a short distance away you'll come to an old, old trail that takes off to the left and goes over to Lost Lake. I believe there's a sign there now where this trail branches off. It's about two miles to Lost Lake. If you can cross the creek at the inlet of Lost Lake, the trail climbs out then swings around to the north. It goes up Moya Canyon a ways then turns away to the east and goes about a mile on the left of a lake and joins the Highline Trail at the Upper Fremont Crossing.

Back at Seneca Lake you follow the main trail around Little Seneca Lake (another ledge to climb during highwater). Under some ledges past the lake you'll see a little spring coming from under a ledge and running across the trail. This is clear, cold water and very refreshing to drink. It's the best in the range.

You continue on over a little hump and on to the next lake (Julie Lake) where you'll join the Highline Trail. Going to the right you'll climb gradually a ways, pass between Debbie and two other lakes then climb to Lester Pass. After descending from the pass you'll pass between Lake Nelson on the right and Tommy Lake on your left. There are several lakes near Nelson Lake and all these are full of golden trout. The Highline Trail continues on to the upper Pole Creek crossing then swings south and goes down to Pole Creek Lakes. Near the upper crossing the Fremont Trail comes and joins the Highline Trail, having come up from the south.

Back near Little Seneca Lake the Highline Trail goes north climbing a series of switchbacks to a high saddle. Here you'll see an ancient signboard where the Indian Pass Trail takes off to Island Lake about a mile and a half away. Following the Highline trail to the left, in about three miles you'll reach the upper Fremont Crossing which has a footbridge to get across Fremont Creek.

At the Fremont Crossing the Highline Trail continues on to the northwest where you'll pass Lower Jean Lake in a mile or so and on to Upper Jean Lake a mile above Lower Jean. About a mile above this lake the Shannon Pass trail takes off to Shannon Pass and goes over to Peak Lake (some 2-1/2 miles) from which you can reach Mammouth Glacier. (See elsewhere in this guide for information on this area and for continuing on the Highline Trail to Elbow Lakes (golden trout), Summit Lake, and on to Green River Lakes.)

Fremont Peak over Lost Lake

INDIAN PASS TRAIL

The Indian Pass Trail takes off from the Highline Trail above Little Seneca Lake, goes around Island Lake, into the lower end of Titcomb Basin, climbs out to the right up into Indian Basin and goes on to end at Indian Pass on the Continental Divide. From the pass, you can wander out on the glaciers on the other side but there are no trails. If you're not a mountain climber or a glacier hiker you'll turn around and come back at the pass.

Indian Basin has no fish but it is a very scenic area. People hike in here just to see the peaks and cliffs all around there. The trail probably got its name because the Indians used to come through the pass many years ago. It's a well-worn trail part way with no signboards.

Fremont Peak can be climbed best from Indian Basin. You climb to the South Ridge and follow the ridge on up to the summit.

Jackson Peak can also be climbed from Indian Basin. You go on around to the far side of the basin and up the stream to the highest lake. Here the route takes off to the north and goes right up into a gash, up a gulley up into the ledges to the right of the peak just ahead of you. When you get above the cliffs and ledges it's all ice. You can walk right up the ice clear to the summit at 13,517 feet with ropes and ice axes.

A glacier hike can be made going through Indian Pass onto the east side of the divide. Only experienced climbers should try it and then using ropes, crampons and ice axes as it's extremely dangerous. A route that one can follow over the glaciers goes out onto Knife Point Glacier, swinging around to the left up onto Bull Lake Glacier. Then you climb up to Upper Fremont Glacier north of Fremont Peak, continue north past Mt. Sacagawea onto Sacagawea Glacier, on to Helen Glacier. You go around the right of Turret Peak and up to Backpackers Pass where you have to turn around and come back because you can't go down the other side of the pass. Most climbers now call it Suicide Pass.

As you near Island Lake, you'll descend a little then come to a nice place to camp overlooking the lake. There is no firewood here as people have broken off everything all around to use for a fire. There are a few trees but nothing for campfire. You go around the east end of the lake, cross a little creek coming down from a lake up above. There are no fish up there. Going up that creek you can make your way to the top of Mount Lester at 12,342 feet, but it's not easy. A good view point lower down at 11,448 feet is easier to reach and is above the Indian Pass trail on the right before you get to Island Lake. From this point you can look north west up Fremont Creek, past both Jean Lakes. From Mount Lester you can see through Shannon Pass and see the top of Squaretop Mountain above Green River Lakes. Also from the top you can look back to the southwest and see Fremont Lake. Also you can see Lost Lake, Seneca Lake and Willow Lake, among others. Up Titcomb Canyon you can see six Titcomb Lakes and of course all the peaks along the Continental Divide north and east of you.

We don't stop hiking because we grow old, we grow old because we stop hiking.

Finis Mitchell

Upper Fremont Glacier, largest of the Bull
Lake Glacier System

TITCOMB LAKES TRAIL

From Island Lake you climb a little to
get into the lower end of Titcomb Basin at a
lake. You go around the hill in a grassy
place to a signboard showing where the
Titcomb Lakes trail begins. Normally until
late in August, people have to go upstream
where it's under the rocks to get across the
stream.

The Titcomb Lakes Trail continues right
up the valley past all the lakes and stops
about a half mile beyond the farthest lake.
Using Titcomb Basin as a base camp, mountain
climbers climb the peaks to the east and
north: Fremont Peak, Mt. Sacagawea, Mt.
Helen, Mt. Warren, Dinwoody Peak, Miriam Peak

and Bobs Towers. Leaving the Continental Divide and coming around the top of the basin, they climb the Titcomb Needles, Twin Peaks and Split Mountain above Peak Lake. From the trail's end above the upper lake, you can climb across the rocks and on up to Dinwoody Pass, which is one of the main routes in to climb Gannett Peak.

GANNETT PEAK FROM DINWOODY PASS ROUTE

Go up through Dinwoody Pass which will almost always be in snow. Then if you want to go to Gannett Peak, go right on over. There is a little spring right over this summit under some rocks. Go down on to Dinwoody Glacier on the left. Cross over to Gooseneck Pinnacle ridge and right there on the ridge is the only safe place for a high camp. There are rock walls piled up around the tent spots to keep the wind from ripping them off the ropes.

The simplest and most direct route to the top is to follow up the left side of Gooseneck Glacier part way, then when you encounter the Bergschrunds where the glacier is broken up, climb onto Gooseneck Pinnacle ridge and follow it up to the divide. Follow right up the ridge onto the ice and to the top of Gannett Peak, the highest peak in Wyoming at 13,804 feet. Crampons ropes and ice axe are needed to make this climb and should be used for safety whenever you're out on steep glaciers. There is another route coming up Dinwoody Creek but the last part of the climb up Gooseneck Glacier uses the same route. This is the easiest and safest route to the top.

Also up at the head of Titcomb Basin there is a route coming through Knapsack Col

White-capped Gannet Peak, looking from
Jackson Peak

from Peak Lake. These directions are
included in the Green River Lakes - Peak Lake
section of this guide.

Many people who are not climbers come
into the Titcomb Basin to catch golden trout.
The Titcomb Lakes had no fish in them until
ten or twelve years ago. The waters are
milky with glacial flour. Golden trout were
planted in Mistake Lake by mistake, hence its
name. These goldens have grown to around
three and a half pounds and people come in
just to fish for them. The fish migrated
downstream to spawn and have since spread
into all the Titcomb Lakes. Mistake Lake
lies about a quarter mile to the east, about
200 feet higher than the main Titcomb Lakes.
There is no trail to it - you just go to the
upper Titcomb Lake to the lower end where a

stream comes down from the right. Follow up this stream. There are fish spawning places in the spring along here. Mistake Lake sits up on a shelf above the other lakes at the base of Fremont Peak. The entire Titcomb Basin is in a deep canyon where on the right the walls rise from the lake at 10,575 feet to Fremont Peak at 13,745 feet. On the left it's worse only not as high, up to 12,450 feet.

PINE CREEK CANYON TRAIL

The Pine Creek Canyon Trail begins right at the campground. There's a turntable in the parking area which you go through. The trail leads right down the hill north, crosses Faler Creek and zig-zags downward for about a mile and a half to the lower end of Long Lake.

Long Lake is in the Wilderness Area so no motors are allowed. It can be reached by going down the Pine Creek Canyon Trail a little over a mile to the outlet. Crossing Fremont Creek to get on the north side of Long Lake can be dangerous. If you want to go on the other side it's better to go on down Fremont to the bridge and come back up.

From the Upper Fremont Lake Campground (accessible only by boat) some people carry rubber rafts up to Long Lake to fish. (It's about a mile away and up about 450 feet.) Then some carry the rafts from the upper end of the lake across a short distance up to Upper Long Lake and can go clear to the end of it.

There's a lot of fish in these lakes. The lakes are very scenic, sitting in a long gorge with two thousand foot cliffs on either side. You can fish up Fremont Creek about a half mile but the gorge closes in and you can go no further. That's how come the lake on up from here below Gorge Lake is named Suicide Lake. I named that back in 1952 when I climbed and fell part way getting to it and had to leave part of my equipment there to get out. It is still there as far as I know. I'm not going after it.

From the outlet of Long Lake the Pine Creek Canyon Trail descends gradually on down Fremont Creek and crosses on a footbridge where Pine Creek comes in. Here you start about a two mile climb, up 2,000 feet to Glimpse Lake. Here the Glimpse Lake Trail joins from the left (west). The Glimpse Lake Trail is a far easier way to get to this lake and points north because you don't have to climb down two thousand feet, then climb back up two thousand feet to get to Glimpse Lake as you do on the Pine Creek Canyon Trail. (See the Spring Creek Park Entrance description for this trail.)

From Glimpse Lake, the trail climbs gradually on to the north, passing Prospector Lake (off trail) in about a half mile then Little Trapper Lake in another mile and a half (no fish here). Trapper Lake is only a short distance further. The Section Corner Lake Trail joins here from the west. Going on north you pass Trail Lake. From here you can detour over to Neil Lake and rejoin the main trail at Gottfried Lake. At Trail and Gottfried Lakes trails take off to the left over to Heart Lake which has rainbow trout. All these other lakes near here contain cutthroats. From Gottfried you continue on to Borum Lake which is only a couple of miles from Summit Lake where the trail ends as it joins the Highline Trail. A good loop route from Summit Lake would take you west to Palmer Lake, south to Section Corner Lake, east to Trapper Lake where you're back on the Pine Creek Canyon Trail.

Another main loop is go south from Summit Lake. From the southeast corner of the lake you take the trail that goes down and crosses Pine Creek just below the lake. There are a lot of signs at the lake and they are somewhat confusing, so be sure to take the one that crosses Pine creek, following the Highline Trail. This goes over to Elbow Lake, Upper Jean, Lower Jean, Island Lake, Little Seneca Lake where you leave the Highline Trail and get on the Seneca Lake Trail. Go down to Seneca Lake, on to Hobbs Lake, Barbara and join the Pole Creek Trail near Eklund Lake. Following west on this trail will take you back to Elkhart Park. This entire loop can be done in four days but you should have five or six.

GLACIER TRAIL

On the little divide above and between Upper Jean and Elbow Lake there's a sign that says "Glacier Trail." This goes through Shannon Pass at 11,150 feet. (The pass was named for a deceased forest ranger.) You can still get a horse down the switchbacks on the other side to Peak Lake. You go around, cross the outlet on the north side and there's a trail that goes around the rock slide (unless it has slid in again) and goes on about a mile for horses, and from there you're afoot. This is where people go onto Mammouth Glacier. (This used to be called Green River Glacier.) Some people use Mammouth Glacier as a route to climb Gannet Peak. This is not the best route and only experienced climbers should try it from this side. To get onto the glacier, you climb through the pass to the left of Split

60

Mountain then out onto the glacier.

On the west side of Peak Lake, there's a signboard pointing up west to Dale Lake. This is a horse trail leading through Cube Rock Pass to the lake. A horse can go on past the lake and a short distance down Green River but no further. Rock slides have closed this area for horses. Hikers can make their way through the slides for about a mile and pick up the trail on the west side of the river that leads up over Vista Pass and down to the Highline Trail on Trail Creek. (This Peak Lake explained previously for people out of Green River Lake Entrance. Here it is explained again for people out of Elkhart Park Entrance when west of Island Lake.)

There is a horse trail from a couple of miles below Summit Lake that takes off from the Highline Trail and goes to Sauerkraut Lakes and on into the Bridger Lakes area and ends. It begins above Pass Lake and goes through Gunsight Pass down to Sauerkraut Lakes, about a mile away. Continuing on past the west end of these lakes you climb a ways then swing to the east across Cumberland Creek, climb the other side, then swing south about another mile to one of the largest of the Bridger Lakes. From here there are no more trails but you can use a contour map and make your way among the forty or so lakes in this area. You can climb around these mountains and every hole has a lake in it. Little has been said about Big Elbow Lake and its Goldens on the Highline Trail between Upper Jean and Pass Lakes. Ice usually breaks up about July 15 exposing some of Wyoming's largest Golden trout, some growing to 8 pounds.

MEADOW LAKE ENTRANCE

Trails: Timico Lake, Bell Lakes

U.S.G.S. Maps: Fayette Lake, Horseshoe Lake, Fremont Peak South

The Timico Lake Trail actually leads from Meadow Lake, after bearing right around locked aluminum gate, as explained below. It goes to the Belford Lakes, three Jacquline Lakes, Barnes and Timico Lakes, and via connecting trails, to both Spruce Lakes, Junction, Chain, 1000 Island, Pole Creek Lakes, Bell and Baldy Lakes, a dozen lakes in Bald Mountain Basin, the Cooks, Nelson and Wall Lakes. As for hot fishing, in my opinion it rates highest along with Dry Creek and St. Lawrence Basin Entrances.

No map, Forest, or Highway sign lists this as an entrance anywhere, perhaps because it is the principle access to two commercial outfitters on Meadow and Burnt lakes, but I'll tell you how to get there without tresspassing.

Exactly .9 mile past the Boulder Store and Post Office on U.S. 191 going toward Pinedale, at a cattle guard, a big Forst Service sign reads: Burnt Lake Road--Boulder Lake Dam 7, Bridger National Forest 10, Burnt Lake 11, Meadow Lake 13.

This is a good graded road with no gates (all cattle guards) right to Meadow Lake, all inside your National Forest after it crosses Fall Creek on a bridge just below Burnt Lake.

The private property at Meadow Lake is fenced and has an aluminum gate that is chained and padlocked. This property and most of the lake is all on the Bridger National Forest and outside the private property fence the road ends at the lake with

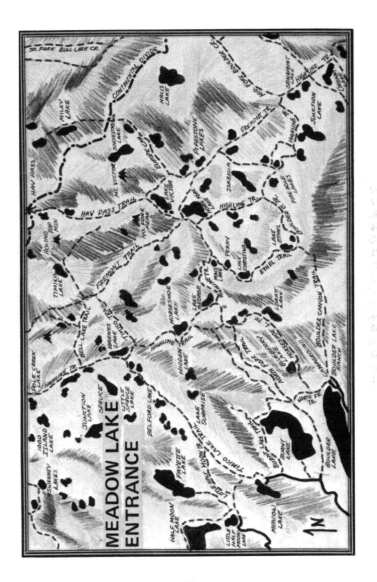

63

plenty of parking space, all on your own forest. In fact, if people only knew it, they couldn't drive their car much further anyway.

TIMICO LAKE TRAIL

About 100 feet back from the locked gate a trail leaves the road to the right very plain and deep worn by cattle, horses, and game animals. It leads into the timber right around the corner of the fence and all outside the fence to its next corner where the fence turns west. But the trail goes right on about 400 feet and drops down to Meadow Creek where several old board tent frames are used by the commercial outfitter. Here you step across the tiny creek and a hundred feet to the left an old road comes out of a wire gate and leads up the mountain to an old sawmill setting and here the Timico Trail begins.

About two miles on, the Little Half Moon Trail joins this Timico Lake Trail, one mile before they enter the Bridger Wilderness boundary. This is much better and shorter than the Half Moon trails anyway. Inside the wilderness they pass the old Black's Cabin at Belford Lake, two unnamed ones, Lake Jacquline and other small ones. Just before it reaches Barnes Lake it joins the Highline Trail where forest signs read: Meadow Lake Trail--Meadow Lake 10, Little Half Moon Lake 11, Highline Trail-- Chain Lakes 2, Pole Creek 4, Horseshoe Lake 3, North Fork Lake 9.

Less than a mile east the Timico Lake Trail turns left off the Highline Trail and up Fall Creek some three miles to the Fremont Trail, follows it back west less than one mile where the Bell Lakes Trail crosses the

Fremont Trail and both lead 1-1/2 miles
northeast to Timico Lake. Timico is a large
lake full of cutthroat trout and sets in a
glacial cirque just under the continental
divide. It's not steep getting to it but
unless you return the same way you went in,
you must climb to a high saddle south of
Round Top Mountain then descend to the North
Fork of Boulder Creek. Then crossing the
stream, (North Fork of Boulder Creek) you
pick up the Hay Pass Trail, explained later.

BELL LAKES TRAIL

Back at Barnes Lake, if one follows the
Highline Trail 2 miles to Chain Lake
(although no maps show it) turn to the left
and cross the stream between this Chain Lake
and Big Spruce Lake where a horse trail
follows downstream on the rightside past
Little Spruce Lake and on down to Junction
Lake on Pole Creek proper, about three miles
above Fayette Lake down near the Half Moon
lakes.

Back at Lower Chain Lake on the Highline
Trail near this lake's inlet the Bell Lakes
Trail turns back east to the right, crosses
Baldy Creek and straight on across Fremont
Trail and again to Timico Lake as on Timico
Lake Trail described before. Or, right after
it crosses Baldy Creek a left turn follows
Baldy Creek to its head where it also joins
Fremont Trail, leading over a pass into Pole
Creek below the Cook Lakes.

Again back at the Chain Lakes the
Highline Trail leads past all the Chain Lakes
to the Lower Pole Creek Crossing, then
upstream to the Cook Lakes as described
earlier on Pole Creek Trail from Elkhart Park
to Ecklund Lake and this same Lower Pole
Creek Crossing.

BOULDER LAKE ENTRANCE

Trails: Boulder Canyon, North Fork,
Horseshoe Lake, Hay Pass, Fremont

U.S.G.S. Maps: Scab Creek, Horseshoe Lake,
Fremont Peak South, Alpine Lakes, Halls
Mountain.

Horseshoe Lake Trail goes to Lovatt Lake,
Cross, Coyote and Horseshoe Lake to join the
Highline Trail which goes on to Chain Lakes
and beyond. North Fork Trail goes to Coyote
Lake and across to Lake George to join the
Highline Trail. Boulder Canyon Trail goes up
Boulder Canyon and Pipestone Creek to Vera
Lake and joins the Highline Trail.   Lake
Ethel Trail leaves the Boulder Canyon Trail
at North Fork Falls, runs past Lake Ethel,
Lake Christina, Perry Lake and joins the
Highline Trail at Macs Lake.
Both the Boulder Canyon Trail and the
North Fork Trail start at the Boulder Lake
Campground. To get there you start at the
Boulder Store and turn east off U.S. 191 on a
paved road.   Signs at this corner point to
Boulder Lake Ranch, among other places.
Follow the paved road 2-1/2 miles only and
turn left on a dirt road.   Signs here will
point to Boulder Lake Ranch. It is a good
graded road; leads to Boulder Lake, along the
south side and clear to the end at a fine
public campground. Just around a knob of
rocks is the Boulder Lake Ranch.

*Too many of us follow endless trails.
Unless a trail leads us somewhere and ends,
it is but a circle.*

Valley Lake

NORTH FORK TRAIL

Burnt Lake can again be reached from here by crossing the footbridge near this campground and following the North Fork Trail up on top of a mountain. You've already passed a right turn trail to Blueberry Lake but you go on to the top, cross a horse trail coming from left up the big ridge between Burnt and Boulder lakes, then keep left on down to Burnt Lake. This trail eventually circles west around Burnt Lake and ends at the road near Meadow Lake. However, you can drive to Burnt Lake and Meadow Lakes, remember.

Also, this North Fork Trail is the old original trail leading past Coyote Lake where it joins the present Horseshoe Lake Trail for about a half mile, then bears right and joins the present Highline Trail near Lake George, which it now follows past Edmond Lake, Macs Lake and on to North Fork Lake.

And here, to avoid confusion, the trail which crossed the Burnt Lake Trail previously described is primarily a dude outfit trail. Back on the Burnt Lake Road (where I said it crossed Fall Creek on a bridge just below Burnt Lake) instead of crossing the bridge on Fall Creek, trucks have traveled as far up the ridge to the right as possible and then this hunters and outfitters trail begins where trucks can go no further. It leads up the big ridge between Boulder and Burnt Lakes, crosses the Burnt Lake Trail and leads on up the mountain from 8,600 to 9,600 feet where it joins the Horseshoe Lake Trail about a mile north of Coyote Lake and a mile south of Horseshoe Lake on the present Highline Trail. Both trails lead on to Horseshoe Lake, then on to cross the Timico Lake Trail described in Meadow Lake chapter. This trail is quite confusing. It leads all the way up the mountain from the Fall Creek bridge to Horseshoe Lake, usually about one half mile to the left of the Horseshoe Lake Trail which begins at the Boulder Lake Campground.

HORSESHOE LAKE TRAIL

Now the better Horseshoe Lake Trail beginning at the Boulder Lake campground is the same as the Burnt Lake Trail, but turns right about half way up the big mountain side, goes to Blueberry Lake, crosses the outlet, up past Lovatt Lake, Cross Lake, Coyote Lake and on to join the Highline Trail at Horseshoe Lake, etc.

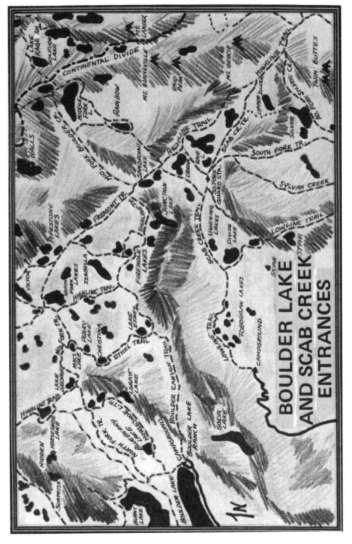

BOULDER LAKE AND SCAB CREEK ENTRANCES

Pleasant Camping at Lake Louise

BOULDER CANYON TRAIL

Again back to the Boulder Lake campground, the Boulder Canyon Trail is like an octopus with twin arms. It starts upstream from the campground but in about 1/4 mile crosses the ranch and follows an old road about a mile, then it goes into the timber and crosses the river on a horse bridge and from there on is on the north (left) side of the river. Some distance above the Still Water Meadows it crosses Macs Creek and right at a massive blue/green pool, the old horse trail turns left and follows Macs Creek to Christina Lake where Ethel Lake Trail joins it. Both go across the creek and on to Perry Lake, join the present Highline Trail at Macs Lake and follow same on to northwest corner of North Fork Lake just below August Lake on Fremont Trail.

Back at the big blue/green pool where we turned up Macs Creek, the Canyon Trail follows on up Boulder Creek and finally bears left up on the hillside above the river, but is soon crowded back to the river at a narrow horse bridge very high above the water. Back 100 feet before the bridge, the Ethel Lake Trail turns up left leading above North Fork Falls to Ethel Lake. It leads along west side of Ethel Lake and heads up a big draw past what your Horseshoe Lake U.S.G.S. Maps shows as Eds Lake, which is nothing but a tiny beaver dam and sometimes is practically dry. A short distance past it a horse trail turns up to the right following the little creek a half mile up to Norman Lakes, with only a beaver run between them, and the trail stops there. They have Golden trout, and you must go back down to the main trail which leads over to Christina Lake on Macs Creek to join the old trail as described up Macs Creek previously.

Back at the horse bridge, high above the stream, the Canyon Trail crosses said bridge, passes Dugway Lake and finally over into Pipestone Creek which it follows to Lake Vera and forks. The trail which doesn't cross the creek at Vera Lake leads along the west side of Lake Vera, leading on westward to and passes Weenona Lake and on to North Fork Lake at the outlet. The best trail from this outfitter's camp goes on along west side of North Fork Lake and after joining the Highline Trail, goes to the northwest corner of North Fork Lake below August Lake.

In wilderness man learns to have faith in his Creator.

Finis Mitchell

HAY PASS TRAIL

Right here it's time to describe the Hay Pass Trail. From this very point it leaves all trails and leads along west side of Victor Lake to the far north end and north inlet, North Fork Creek proper. It crosses the creek and a short distance up trail the stream levels out in a big fine basin where the cutthroat trout have a great spawning bed. However, the trail leads on up through a lot of timber coming out above timberline to Barbara Lake. Remember, back down stream above the spawning grounds, the trail from Timico Lake came down to join the Hay Pass Trail.

From this Barbara Lake the Hay Pass Trail continues on north over the pass, past Dennis Lake and to the Golden Lakes, some call them. They are on the Middle Fork of the great Bull Lake Creek from the glacial region. The golden trout were headed for the Alpine lakes by the Brown Cliffs, but Cris Berg thought he had arrived there so he turned the trout loose in what turned out to be this group of clear lakes. This was a stroke of luck, because if he had taken them to the Alpine Lakes they would have died. They named the upper lake Golden Lake and I named the middle one Lake Louise because it reminded me of this great lake in Canada. However, the Hay Pass Trail leads past these three lakes and does go on over to the Alpine Lake region below the Brown Cliffs where it practically ends at Camp Lake below Douglas Peak in the Brown Cliffs region. From the Alpine Lakes between the Brown Cliffs and the continental divide, one can hike up over a pass and right out on the glaciers leading into Indian Pass described in Elkhart Park Entrance at the head of Indian Basin in Knife Point Peak area. Around from Camp Lake is the big Bull Lake Creek, all milky from seven glaciers.

FREMONT TRAIL

Back at the northwest corner of North Fork Lake where the Hay Pass Trail took off, likewise does the Fremont Trail leading high over Hat Pass, past Rambaud Lake (no fish), above Lake Sequa (fine fishing) on across the Timico and Bell Lakes Trails and into Bald Mountain Basin and to the Cook Lakes. This basin has some 14 lakes and above Upper Cook Lake is Wall Lake, now with two to three pound goldens. It can be reached easy from the Pole Creek Trail, Highline Trail above the Chain Lakes or over a pass east of Island Lake (no trail).

Again on this great octopus, at Lake Vera the Canyon Trail crosses the creek at Lake Vera and leads off east to the Fire Lakes, on up past Lake Isabelle, upstream past Howard Lake to the Pipestone Lakes on the old Highline Trail. Both Pipestone lakes have been great cutthroat fishing. Up the stream above Upper Pipestone lake to the east is Lake Prue, where at one time I caught eight pound cutthroats. On north of the Pipestone lakes is Valley Lake (no fish). A horse trail (the original Hay Pass Trail) passes Valley Lake on the right side. Right on a little saddle where an old trappers cabin sits, a trail takes off to the east (right), leadingup into the Europe Canyon Lakes, all having great cutthroat trout in them. This same trail at the cabin north of Valley Lake leads right on past Victor Lake on the east side, joining the now Hay Pass Trail right near the big spawning beds on North Fork Creek. There's still a bit more to the octopus which will be in next chapter.

The massive Middle Fork Lake

SCAB CREEK ENTRANCE

U.S.G.S. Maps: Scab Creek,   Raid Lake, Mt.
Bonneville, Halls Mountain, Roberts Mountain.

Lowline Trail goes up through the
Toboggan Lakes to the Divide Lake country.
Branching south it goes into the Silver Lakes
country, mainly past Big Divide Lake to
Monroe and Star Lakes. Scab Creek Trail
begins at Divide Lake and goes into the
Bonneville Basin past the South Fork Guard
Station and joins the Highline Trail above
Cross Lake. From the South Fork Guard
Station trails take off in all directions; to
Wolf Lake, Silver Lake, Big Sandy Openings,
East Fork River, Rainbow Lake, Middle Fork
Lake, Raid, Cross, and Dream Lakes, Fire Hole

Lakes, Pipestone Lakes, Sandpoint, and JunctionLakes.

To reach this entrance turn east on paved road off U.S. 191 at Boulder Store. Go six miles on the paved road to several Government buildings on left side. Some 500 feet beyond here, a dirt road turns off the paved road to the left. This is your road. Stay to left all the way on this BLM road to its end at a little campground with space to park cars. This is the entrance.

Now, since private property owners have blocked access to this area for the public, the following trails into the Bridger National Forest have long been abolished: Mitchell Cutoff, Sage Basin, Silver Creek, Chimney Butte, Cottonwood Creek, and worst of all, the Pocket Creek Road which led to Wolf Lake, the Cow Camp and the Silver Lake Dam. Hence, I will describe this chapter as "South" and "North". Don't follow any of these trails out where signed.

From the campground the trail climbs up a hill to join the Old Lowline Trail, up and past Toboggan Lakes and finally to Little Divide Lake by an old canal bringing water from Big Divide Lake over into the Scab Creek drainage. Here the trail forks, one south, one north.

South Portion

First I'll describe the South portion of the area where the main lakes are blocked from direct access. Head south along right side of Big Divide Lake, all in timber. It has rainbow trout. As the trail leaves the southeast point of Big Divide, it leads through a mild pass and soon to Monroe Lake. Here a heavy cow trail leads along the hillside to the right and down Monroe Creek, but not for you. Go on past Monroe Lake on the right side across the outlet. At the far south end an old sign should still be pointing east up the Mitchell Cutoff Trail which leads northeast to the South Fork Basin.

To proceed further into this blocked-access area go straight on south to Star Lake which usually has two to three pound brooks. The trail passes it on the left, down into the main Silver Creek, crosses and climbs out on top and over to South Fork of Silver Creek in which most of the water comes out of Wolf Lake underneath an old dam. It has been famous for rainbow trout.

From Wolf Lake go back down to the main stream and follow the Cottonwood Creek Trail up past the Cow Camp (maybe burned down now) and on up stream to Jessie and further to the big Silver Lake. Turn to the right and you'll finally reach the highline Trail at base of Mt. Geikie. If you followed this Highline Trail east you'd go down and cross East Fork River on a sheep bridge, climb out and pass Marms and Dads Lakes and on past Mirror Lake and to the Big Sandy Openings. You can go back to the area from the Sandy Openings via the Lowline or Chilcoot Trails.

Back at the Silver Lake Dam if you follow the left shore on past Upper Silver Lake and through a pass you come to Cross Lake and the Highline Trail again.

Again back at the old Cow Camp the South Fork Trail heads straight north, passes Shoestring Lake (no fish) and crosses the main Silver Creek at the second lake below the Silver Lake Dam and leads north to the South Fork Guard Station.

Crescent Lake Brook Trout

    And back at Wolf Lake when you follow the outlet down to the main stream, directly across it a heavy cow trail leads straight north up a slowly climbing draw and over to cross the main Silver Creek about 2-1/2 miles below the Silver Lake Dam. Then follow the North Fork of Silver Creek up past Knob Lake where it joins the South Fork Trail and both go to the South Fork Guard Station as before.

    From the Silver Lake Dam all the way downstream to the rapids it has many, many little lakes and pools which are all good fishing. Through this area the closer one gets to the peaks the more open country you find so you can walk about anywhere you wish. Just don't try to follow any Silver Creek drainage or trails out of the mountains because they are all blocked by the ranches.

North Portion

Now, for the North portion of the area, back at Little Divide Lake, on your left cross a swampy patch next to a rocky point, follow a trail along the left shore to the outlet. From here down the tiny creek less than a mile is what I named Pine Island Lake. It's a fine lake with an island covered with pine trees. It sometimes has two pound brooks in it. Nothing further down but a tiny lake with no fish.

Back at the outlet of Little Divide Lake, cross the creek and follow the trail past Lightening Lakes (no fish) and in some three miles it comes out into the great Boulder and Bonneville Basin region. In it are over 60 lakes and all of any size have trout.

Take five here, sit down, relax, and ponder over your U.S.G.S. Mt. Bonneville Map. You've just read about the south area to Wolf Lake and all the Silver Creek drainages. Now rest your eyes on this map as far north as Halls and Middle Fork lakes and to the high peaks on the horizon. In my opinion, neither Dictator nor King has a more divine land elsewhere on the globe. And until about the last 30 years, it's been used mainly for cattle and sheep grazing. Raid Peak just south of Bonneville, and Raid Lake in the center of the basin were named in memory of the vicious sheep raids here, over the range.

Satisfied? Then follow this trail on past the old guard station at the right of heavy timbered area where soon afterwards a trail branches to the left, crosses the stream and leads across the open meadow to join the Highline Trail between Raid and Dream lakes. Or go on, passing South Fork Lake on the left and still further on, Raid

Storm coming over Crescent Lake

Lake down to your left and arrive at Cross Lake where once sat a little white Patrol Cabin, but which I think has been removed since creation of the Bridger Wilderness Area. Your trail goes on to join the Highline Trail beyond this point and Cross Lake.

From this point one can cross-country to the left of Mt. Bonneville to many lakes which drain into Raid Lake via both Raid and South Fork Creeks. This is the original Highline Trail that passes Raid Lake on the east side, then Dream Lake, Bobs, Sandpoint lakes, crosses Halls Creek, on past Pipestone Lakes and to North Fork Lake described previously.

Back where you came into the big park country, a heavy trail in the foreground crosses the big stream (South Fork Boulder

Creek) and eventually goes to Middle Fork Lake. However, right down to your left around the bend in the river a small creek empties into the big stream on the opposite side. Just up on a bench as you look north, it comesfrom Crescent Lake with fine brooks.

A little further up the big stream, Dream Creek also joins it from the north. This deep trail follows the left side of Dream Creek past Dream Lake. Follow around Dream Lake on the left side to its inlet, then follow the inlet (on left) until you reach Rainbow Lake. Follow the horse trail built through the rock slide along the left shore to the far north end. Here a fair trail leads straight north over a nice saddle and down to the creek below MIddle Fork Lake. But you follow your trail on around the lake and a long ways up northeast to a saddle and down to the inlet of the massive Middle Fork Lake. Upstream to the right above Middle Fork is Noel Lake near Nylon and Bonneville peaks. It has fine brooks.

Around Middle Fork Lake near the north inlet, a horse trail leads up a big hill to Bewmark Lake and two unnamed ones above it. We stocked them with trout but they failed to make it. At their outlet a trail, now blocked with rock slides, used to climb to the continental divide here and down into St. Lawrence Basin on the Indian Reservation where there are about 30 lakes. Information on thesewill be in another chapter.

All this Middle Fork river from Noel Lake to Junction Lake above the white waters is great fishing. A heavy trail follows on the north side down Middle Fork to the Highline Trail at Sandpoint Lake where you can cross on a sheep bridge and go back to Dream Lake where you began. But it also goes on down to Junction Lake, the confluence of Middle Fork and Halls Creek. Up Halls Creek where the Highline Trail crosses, a horse trail follows upstream and forks near timberline. The left fork goes to Halls Lake above timberline, and unnamed ones above. They are just over a pass from the Europe Canyon, described in another chapter. The right fork leads across open country to Middle Fork Lake again.

Then from Halls Creek the old Highline Trail goes up past Howard and to Pipestone lakes. From Lower Pipestone a horse trail goes back to the left down a draw to Howard and Isabelle lakes, over to the Fire Lakes where it joins the Highline Trail, and back to Lake Vera. Also from the Fire Lakes this trail goes on over past our Twin Lakes and to Junction Lake and back upstream to the Highline Trail at Sandpoint Lake and a sheep bridge.

There was a forest fire in this area and when it was put out this group of lakes was discovered. We named the prettiest one with a high rock island in it Lake Susan, and another one deep in the woods, Wilderness Lake. Then two others very close together we called the Twin Lakes. My only brother, Dennis, packed fish into the mountains and stocked the whole group. They were all great fishing and because no one knew about them for years, when they did find them, the whole group was dubbed "The Fire Lakes". Hence, the name used to this day.

Back out in the basin, Sunrise Lake empties into Dream Creek and lake. Raid Creek enters Raid Lake in the center of the east side. South Fork, which heads at the foot of Mt. Bonneville, enters at the far north corner. Middle Fork and South Fork joins as one stream a mile below Junction Lake. The Bonneville lakes are at the head of South Fork.

Looking from Big Sandy Pass over Arrowhead
Lake to both Temple Peaks

BIG SANDY ENTRANCE

Trails: Highline, Big Sandy, Lowline, East
Fork

U.S.G.S. Maps: Big Sandy Openings, Mount
Bonneville, Raid Lake, Halls Mountain, Temple
Peak, Lizard Head Peak, Roberts Mountain.

Highline Trail begins here and runs north
to Dads, Marms, Raid, Firehole, North Fork,
George, Horseshoe, Chain, Island, Jean,
Elbow, Summitt, and down to Green River Lakes
Entrance. Big Sandy Trail goes to Big Sandy
Lake where it branches to go on up to Cirque
of the Towers, up Rapid Creek to Temple Peak
and down Little Sandy. Lowline Trail runs
over to Poston Meadows, Poston Lake and up to

Wolf Lake and beyond. East Fork Trail begins at Poston Meadows and runs up East Fork River to the Highline Trail.

Washakie Trail runs north from Marms Lake up to Washakie Pass and beyond. Chilcoot Trail runs from the East Fork Trail below Boulter Lake past Chilcoot Lake past Cow Camp to join the Lowline Trail in the Silver Creek drainage.

This all begins in the Big Sandy Openings, well on the southern end of the range. There are four ways to get to it.

From the Boulder Store on U.S. 191 you take the only road (oiled) leading out of there off U.S. 191. It heads east. When the oiled road ends, just keep going on the main road, to the left all the time, never right. It heads into the mountains, passes the Dutch Joe Guard Station and goes on to the Big Sandy Openings. Clear at the far north end, cross the river on a new bridge (built 1974), and turn right to the campground. If you turn left at the bridge, it ends around the corner by Mud Lake at the Big Sandy Lodge where we set up our tent in 1930. (Now at Mud Lake there is a fine lodge and ten cabins for those not wishing to use the campground.)

Another route is 73.2 miles north of Rock Springs on U.S. 191, turn right at a Forest Service sign reading "Big Sandy Entrance". This is Muddy Speedway, a fine dirt road. Stay right on it all the way to the Big Sandy river bridge. Stay left from there on as from Boulder way.

Another route from U.S. 191 is at Farson, a small town 41 miles from Rock Springs. Turn east on Wyo. 28 and at about 2-1/2 miles or possibly 3, a big sign board reads Big Sandy Entrance and many others. Turn left on this dirt road, following road signs again to Big Sandy Entrance (Openings).

The fourth route is from Lander on U.S. 287. Seven miles south of Lander stay right on Wyo. 28 until you cross the Sweetwater bridge. One mile past the bridge more signs turn you right on a dirt road again. This road is marked as the Old Lander Trail, with government metal signs all along it. Follow it until you cross Little Sandy River and on to the next stream. This is Squaw Creek, but .3 mile before you get to its bridge there are four signs telling you everything with distances, so you turn right and go on to the Big Sandy Entrance as on the other routes.

The Big Sandy Openings is the most popular entrance to the Wind River Range. It is where we started our Mitchell's Fishing Camp back in 1930 amongst the sheep and cattle, but which has now grown into a great recreation region. It is where we went to the end of the sheep wagon road and set up our tent, and packed 2-1/2 million tiny trout in milk cans on horses, and stocked 314 virgin mountain lakes where the people are enjoying their public lands today.

HIGHLINE TRAIL

The Highline Trail starts here at the campground and leads clear along the continental divide to the Green River Lakes on the other end of the Bridger Wilderness. Occasionally a group hikes this entire trail, maybe not every summer, but once in a while. The portion that they use now is about 100 miles long. It would take about a week for average hikers. When people ask me how long it might take I tell them that young people should do it in about five days. That's about 20 miles a day. But you're not walking 100 miles around a golf course or a city park at 4,000or 6,000 feet above sea level. At 10- to 12,000 feet up it's different. Out on the level at 6,000 feet I can walk 40 miles in 14 hours, but at 11,000 feet and with 50 to 60 pounds on your back it's something else. And, on a trip like this it isn't a marathon, you're there to enjoy the land as God intended. So I tell them they should take Sunday to Sunday, six work days and two to play.

If you're going to hike the entire Highline Trail, it's much better to start at the Big Sandy Openings, because you're already at 8,190 feet to start with. If you start at the Green River Lakes Entrance at 7,961 feet you have to climb to 11,055 feet where you start down to the Jean Lakes and Fremont Crossing, then climb back to 11,090 feet at Lester Pass. Just don't expect an easy trail, because it's not there. But if that's what people like, I agree with them, I've been at it 66 years since my dad started me climbing. I'd like to climb 'till I'm 90.

At the Big Sandy Campground, both the Big Sandy and Highline Trails start together at the road's end in camp. About one half mile along the riverbank in timber, you come into a park to a box for registering. Less than another half mile on the river bank is a sign board and the trail forks. The Highline Trail goes left and the Big Sandy Trail goes right, along the river. The sign gives directions and distances (Big Sandy Lake 6, Dads Lake 5).

On the Highline Trail to Dads Lake, in another mile you come to Meeks Lake. It is on your left and on the other side is the original Highline Trail. Here, there is another sign "Big Sandy Lake 5 and Dads Lake 4."

The side trail to Big Sandy Lake passes V

Lake which has big rainbows, but the local people usually get most of them when the ice goes out. The trail goes on past Diamond Lake and just beyond it joins the regular Big Sandy Trail.

Continuing on the Highline Trail from the sign board mentioned above, you must cross the little creek and go over to the big horse trail where it goes up a steep, sandy hill. A hundred yards up the hill a big sign says "Bridger Wilderness". The Trail goes up through timber a big two miles to come out in Fish Creek Meadows. Here you look miles north to the big mountains on horizon.

This trail is 8 or 10 inches deep and has been used 99 years by millions of sheep and thousands of horses, and still is. A half mile on, a tiny creek comes down from the right. Barely out of sight in the timber is a little lake people call Divide Lake. It has brook trout in it.

Farther on you come to Fish Creek. On the south side of the creek a trail leads down to Francis Lake. It is always good fishing, especially for kids. Fish Lake, Mirror, Dads, Donald, Marms, Elizabeth and the little Divide lakes all drain into Francis Lake. However, a trail goes through the timber up to Fish Lake if you can find it. Fish Lake is right at timberline and the head of Fish Creek. Nothing above but Fish Creek Pass.

Back where the Highline (stock) Trail crosses Fish Creek you go up a little hill to Mirror Lake, which has fish in it sometimes. They smother some winters. On in another meadow (if you can find it) a trail turns right into the timber and eventually reaches Donald Lake. Again nothing but mountains above.

Now the Highline Trail comes to Dads

Lake. It is only six miles from your car and is quite heavily used, but it's pretty good fishing. The trail leads around the right side, crosses Donald Creek and goes on to Marms Lake.

Marms Lake is about a mile on up from Dads Lake. We put ten thousand brook trout in it and there was only food for about two thousand so they never did get very big but they're still there, about ten inches long now. At the far northwest corner two signs are on a post. One says Washakie Pass 5 and Haley Pass 6.

Taking the Highline Trail you go 1-1/2 or 2 miles to East Fork river. You can wade it, or downstream a half mile is a sheep bridge. (Sheep have to have a bridge but nobody worries about hikers.) If you cross the bridge and follow the Highline Trail 2-1/2 miles up-hill it gets to the Silver Creek drainage and farther to Cross Lake, described in the Scab Creek Entrance.

Or (there is little or no trail) after crossing the river you can go upstream to the left to the East Fork Lakes above timberline. They were stocked with goldens but I think most of them came downstream. No trail.

Now back at the sign post at Marms Lake both the Washakie and Hailey Pass trails are one. It is about two miles to Washakie Creek where you may have to go upstream a mile to get across. Here a horse trail goes on up this creek two miles, crosses to the north side and on up to Shadow Lake. Go back over to the left to the trail (if you don't find it again just go up the hill to timber line) to Billys Lake, on to Barren Lake, (no trail beyond here) cross the creek and go on to Texas Lake. Texas Pass above to the right leads across into the Cirque of the Towers and down to Lonesome Lake. From Lonesome

Lake if you wish you can go over Big Sandy
Pass to Big Sandy Lake and back to your car
at the campground.

Back down at Washakie Creek (when you get
across it) again follow the Washakie and
Hailey Pass trails north through timber up to
the top of a hill where you see Skull Lake in
front of you. Here a sign on a tree back
under the limbs says Washakie Pass 2 miles,
to the east. Even though Washakie, Macon,
Locklaven and Grave Lakes will be described
later, I'll list them here because many
people like to take this loop trip over one
pass and back the other from Big Sandy
Openings. Just under the pass is Macon Lake
with brook trout. Lake on your right has no
fish. Big one at bottom is Washakie Lake.
Locklaven Lake is over north against big
ledges but poor fishing for browns.

From Washakie Lake if one wishes to make
the loop, follow the trail down from the lake
to the main South Fork of Little Wind River
to a lot of signs on your side of the river.
Go down to the left to the first trail, again
to the left and head up to Grave Lake. Cross
below the outlet. Follow the trail around
the right side, and no kidding, it goes right
up against the granite wall above the rock
slide. Follow it right on up, up into Haley
Pass and back to Skull Lake.

Or, at Skull Lake, if you take the Haley
Pass Trail, cross the outlet of Skull Lake
and head north a mile on a ridge of timber,
out above timberline to Twin Lakes (The
U.S.G.S. Map shows it west of both lakes, but
no way can it be.) It goes across the stream
between the lakes into Hailey Pass, and down
to Grave Lake and on the loop backwards if
you wish. However, from Hailey Pass, right
across to your left past an 1,800-foot wall
is a pretty lake. It is Baptiste Lake and

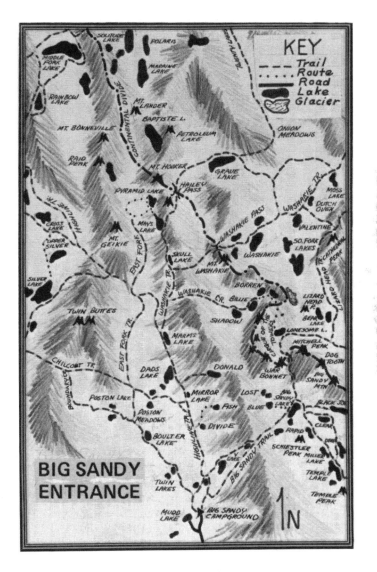

BIG SANDY ENTRANCE

has cutthroats. Only 40 acres at the outlet
is off the Indian Reservation where you can
fish without a permit.

Back down below timberline north of Skull
Lake, a fine lake is down to the west below
the trail. It is Mays Lake where we put the
mackinaws from Grave Lake to stock it in
1933. It drains into East Fork river. It is
fine fishing.

At the far north end of Mays Lake a good
stream enters. A half mile up this stream is
Pyramid Lake with good goldens. From it, (no
trail), you can walk cross-country above
timberline to the East Fork Lakes.

BIG SANDY TRAIL

Going up the Big Sandy River to Big Sandy
Lake you start from the campground and go up
the river a mile where you come to a main
fork in the trail. The Highline Trail goes
to the left, the trail to Big Sandy Lake
leads to the right, crosses Meeks Creek and
follows up Big Sandy River, about six miles
altogether. Thirteen lakes drain into Big
Sandy Lake via five different streams. Blue
Lake and Lost Lake are on Lost Creek from the
west. Arrowhead and Shaft Lake on North
Creek, Black Joe and three unnamed ones on
Black Joe Creek from the east. Deep and
Clear Lake are on Clear Creek. Temple,
Miller and Rapid Lakes are on Rapid Creek
from the southeast. Many people hike into
here and scatter in all directions.

Big Sandy Lake is a popular place for
camping and fishing. There are a lot of
smaller lakes nearby that offer maybe better
fishing and a less crowded experience.
Brookies and some cutthroats in Big Sandy.

Blue Lake is about a mile to the west up

Camping at Lonesome Lake in the Cirque of the
Towers. War Bonnet Peak above.

Lost Creek which is the first stream you
cross while going around Big Sandy Lake.
There is an old trail that works its way
through the trees south of the creek to the
lake. The first lake you reach is Blue Lake.
Some maps call this Lost Lake but Lost Lake
is to be found a short distance to the north
of Blue Lake, on the same stream. Blue Lake
has brook trout in it but there are no fish
in Lost Lake, which sits in a cirque at the

base of Bunion Mountain and War Bonnet.

Black Joe Lake has all cutthroat trout in it. A trail leads up to it starting at the east end of Big Sandy Lake. It's a little over a mile to this long narrow lake which sits at 10,258 feet in a beautiful cirque between the Continental Divide 12,416 and Haystack Mountain 11,978.

Clear Lake and Deep Lake both have brook trout and can be reached on a trail that starts near the east end of Big Sandy Lake. Clear Lake is about a mile, and Deep Lake is about a mile on past the end of Clear Lake. From Deep Lake the trail climbs up to join the Rapid Creek Trail at Temple Lake.

Rapid, Miller, and Temple Lakes all have brook trout and there are some German browns in Temple. These lakes are reached by going up the Rapid Creek Trail which begins at the east end of Big Sandy. It's about a mile to Rapid Lake, less than another mile on to Miller Lake, and just a short way on to Temple Lake which sits in a big cirque at the base of Temple Peak, 12,972. The trail goes on over the pass above Temple Lake (now blocked by mountain slides) and on down Little Sandy Creek past Little Sandy Lake then on out to a road described in the Little Sandy Entrance. Also from Temple Lake you can make a loop over to Deep Lake, back down past Clear Lake to Big Sandy Lake again.

Shaft Lake (North Lake on some maps) and Arrowhead Lakes are reached by following the trail up North Creek which is on the north corner of Big Sandy Lake. This is the trail that leads to Big Sandy Pass and over to Lonesome Lake in the Cirque of the Towers described below and elsewhere in this guide. Arrowhead Lake sits in a deep canyon between War Bonnet Peak at 12,369 feet and Mitchell Peak at 12,482 feet, both on the Continental Divide.

Looking up Titcomb Basin toward Dinwoody Pass

CIRQUE OF THE TOWERS

The famous "Cirque of the Towers" can be reached by going up North Creek from Big Sandy Lake, cross the Continental Divide at Big Sandy Pass (Jackass Pass on some maps) and descend to Lonesome Lake. Here you're in the center of the towers which form a half circle around you to the west, all above twelve thousand feet. Lizard Head Peak is on the north end of the cirque and War Bonnet on the south. Lonesome Lake has good fishing and is the headwaters of the North Fork Popo Agie River. The cirque offers some challenging climbs as all along the east side of these towers it is all sheer cliffs. However, on the opposite sides, a ten year old boy could walk up the slopes to the top

93

Shadow Lake on west side of the Cirque
of the Towers

of some. But from the top, you look two
thousand feet down to the lakes and streams
below you. I had my son on top of War Bonnet
when he was only eleven years old, but we
came up the south side.

A loop trip can be made from the Big
Sandy Campground to Big Sandy Lake, Cirque of
the Towers, cross over Texas Pass to the
Washakie Creek drainage, down past Texas,
Barren, Billys, Shadow Lakes to Marms Lake,
Dads Lake and back to your car at the
campground. To do this, at Lonesome Lake in
the Cirque you can make your way up the
stream that flows from the north into the
west end of the lake. Near the beginning of
the stream you swing a little to the right
and follow up a draw right into Texas Pass on
the divide. Here you'll be overlooking Texas

Lake on the other side. Climb down to and
stay on the left side of Texas and Barren
Lake below it. Cross to the other side of
the stream below Barren Lake. Follow down on
the north side of Billy and Shadow Lakes then
on down Washakie Creek on the south side to
the trail going down to Marms and Dads Lakes
and on south to your car at the Big Sandy
Campground. Horses can't make it over the
divide at the pass but good hikers should
have little trouble.

Lowline and East Fork Trails
    The Lowline and East Fork trails are
seldom used, and quite insignificant because
they only lead back over into the cattle
country, explained in Scab Creek Entrance.

LOWLINE TRAIL

    To get to the head of the Lowline Trail
you have to drive back down the road 2-1/2
miles from the campground to the old sheep
wagon bridge, cross it and follow a very
rocky and usually swampy or boggy road to an
old sawmill setting near Johnson Lake where
it ends. Here the Lowline Trail begins. It
leads about five miles to Boulter Lake
(sometimes poor and sometimes good fishing)
and another mile down to East Fork River.
Here you have to wade the river because the
old sheep bridge is gone now. Directly
across on the other side of the meadow it
heads into the timber, leads up mountains
between Poston Lakes and out on top to
Boundary Creek and beyond to the Cow Camp in
cattle country, explained in the Scab
Entrance.

EAST FORK TRAIL

Off the Lowline Trail after crossing the river this trail leads upstream and eventually joins the Highline Trail near Cross Lake, Scab Creek Entrance. About 1-1/2 miles above the Lowline Trail the Chilcoot Trail leads up a tiny creek (dry after snow gone) past Chilcoot Lake to the Cow Camp and Lowline Trail again.

LITTLE SANDY LAKE ENTRANCE

Trails: Little Sandy Creek

U.S.G.S. Maps: Jensen Meadows, Sweetwater Gap, Temple Peak, Sweetwater Needles

Little Sandy trail goes up Little Sandy Creek to Little Sandy Lake and on up to Temple Peak where it joins the Rapid Creek Trail going down to Big Sandy Lake (not a horse trail). The trail branches at Little Sandy Lake and goes over and down Larsen Creek to the Sweetwater Guard Station.

On Wyoming 28 between Farson and Lander, turn off one mile west of the Sweetwater bridge onto the "Old Lander Trail" road. A big sign there points to Big Sandy Openings, Sweetwater Guard Station and others. Follow this road to the first road which turns off to the right where there's a sign pointing to Sweetwater Guard Station. At the junction follow sign to Block and Tackle Hill. (To the right it is 6 miles to Sweetwater Guard Station.) From here on up you'll need a jeep or four wheel drive to get about four miles to the end of the road near the Wilderness Boundary.

From the road end, it's about four and a half miles of easy gradual climbing up the creek to Little Sandy Lake. Before you reach the lake, the trail branches. The left fork stays on the creek and goes to the outlet of the lake. To the right this trail climbs around south of the lake, crosses the divide and becomes the Little Sandy Trail going down Larson Creek to the road above Sweetwater Guard Station.

The left fork back on Little Sandy Creek below the lake climbs up onto a little bench above the lake and eventually gets back to Little Sandy Creek above the lake.

The trail goes on up the stream climbing gradually for several miles to where it leaves the stream just below the highest of the four Frozen Lakes (no fish). Climbing above this lake you go almost straight up, zig-zagging to a saddle between Temple and East Temple Peaks. Here you cross over and go down to Temple, Miller, Rapid and Big Sandy Lakes. This is not a trail for horses but hikers can make it.

A mountain is the best medicine for a troubled mind. Seldom does man ponder his own insignificance. He thinks he is master of all things. He thinks the world is his without bonds. Nothing could be farther from the truth. Only when he tramps the mountains alone, communing with nature, observing other insignificant creatures about him, to come and go as he will, does he awaken to his own short-lived presence on earth.

Finis Mitchell

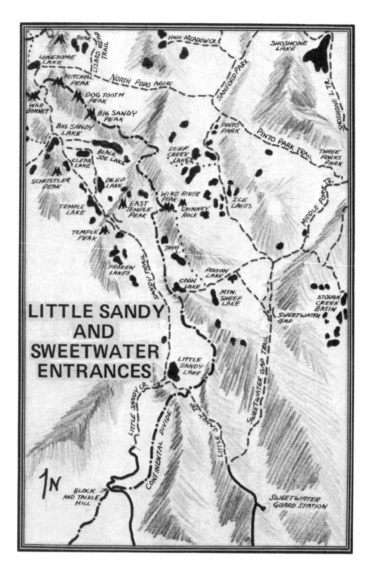

LITTLE SANDY
AND
SWEETWATER
ENTRANCES

SWEETWATER ENTRANCE

Trails: Little Sandy, Sweetwater Gap

U.S.G.S. Maps: Sweetwater Needles, Sweetwater Gap

Little Sandy Trail goes up Larsen Creek to Little Sandy Lake The trail branches at Little Sandy Lake and goes back down the creek to the Little Sandy Entrance. Sweetwater Gap Trail is the main one here and goes up to Sweetwater Gap and on over into the headwaters of Middle Popo Agie River. Over there you can get to Poison, Coon and Toyo Lakes and up to Wind River Peak. Also to the 14 Ice Lakes and 8 Deep Creek Lakes.

The trails start north of the Sweetwater Guard Station.

On Wyoming 28 between Farson and Lander, turn off one mile southwest of the Sweetwater bridge onto the old "Lander Trail" road. Follow big signs all the way to the Sweetwater Guard Station. Just before you reach the guard station you turn left and it's two miles to the end of the road. This two mile stretch is rough for passenger cars but a careful driver can make it. There are no camping facilities at the road end but there is water and places to camp and park cars.

(The guard station is just a little shack and is not occupied. There is a picnic area just south of the station.)

LITTLE SANDY TRAIL

The Little Sandy Trail takes off to the left from the end of the road. It goes up a long slope above Larson Creek to the Continental Divide, climbing about 1300 feet in about four miles. Then it drops rapidly about a half mile to Little Sandy Lake. You can go down the stream to the Block and Tackle road.

SWEETWATER GAP TRAIL

This trail takes off to the right from the end of the road above the Sweetwater Guard Station and it's nine miles to Sweetwater Gap. The trail goes down across Larson Creek then climbs over to follow up the Sweetwater River to it's head. It's not a difficult trail just long gradual climbing to the gap which is a pass 1400 feet higher, overlooking the beginning of the Middle Popo Agie River. Here the Sweetwater Gap Trail ends and the upper end of the Middle Fork Trail begins. This goes on down the river and eventually goes out to Lander.

Right at the gap a heavily used horse trail takes off to the left from the sign boards and into the trees. It goes across fairly level and descends a little to pass just below a small lake on Middle Popo Agie River. Climbing up to the northwest you go through a little saddle then descend to the outlet of Poison Lake on Tayo Creek. There is a campground here for the horse packers. Poison Lake has always been good fishing. The cutthroat and rainbow trout have cross-bred resulting in a hybrid species.

If you're going on up to Coon or Tayo Lakes you can stay above Poison Lake (no

Snow-covered Wind River Peak over Poison
Lake on Tayo Creek

trail) going to the left of it and on up to
Mountain Sheep Lake. There is nice open
camping around this beautiful lake but there
are no fish in it. Near the outlet you cross
over and join the trail coming up from Poison
Lake.

From Poison Lake a horse trail goes up
Tayo Creek and right on up to Coon Lake where
it ends. Golden Trout are in both Coon and
Tayo Lakes.

Tayo Lake can be reached by a route which
takes off to the north from the trail about a
mile below Coon Lake. This goes up on the
left side above the stream then crosses it
after about a half mile. Then stay on the
right of the stream to Tayo Lake.

Wind River Peak can be reached from Tayo
Lake by starting to climb at the east end of

Tayo Lake at the outlet. You start up on a little grassy bald ridge to the right and head north, straight for the big round top mountain ahead of you. Stay on the ridge and head for the snow on the east slope near the saddle east of the summit. It's easier walking on the snow than on the rocks. You won't need crampons as you can kick steps with your hiking boots. Follow the snow right on up to the top.

From the top of Wind River Peak at 13, 192 feet you can look northwest straight along the Continental Divide to Gannett Peak, the highest in Wyoming at 13,804 feet. The Wind River Peak is the highest on the southeastern end of the Wind River Range so you can see all the other peaks from here. Temple Peak is near you almost due west. The sheer walls of East Temple is even closer. Along the divide you see in this order: Big Sandy Peak 13,416, Dog Tooth 12,488, Mitchell 12,482, War Bonnett 12,406, Cirque of the Towers, Lizard Head 12,842 feet.

Also from Sweetwater Gap you can get over into the Deep Creek Lakes and Ice Lakes. Go on the trail down the drainage from the gap for about two miles following the river to where Tayo Creek enters from the left. This will be the first stream entering the Middle Fork Popo Agie River from the left. Find a place to cross and start up Tayo Creek, staying on the right hand side of it. This creek branches very soon and you head up the right branch to the northwest. It looks like you're heading right for Wind River Peak to begin with. This is a horse trail and you can follow it into the cirques of the Ice Lakes and go on to the Deep Creek Lakes. The Ice Lakes contain golden trout and the Deep Creek Lakes have brooks. The Ice Lakes are called such because they are normally frozen up until the fifteenth of July.

In the Deep Creek Lakes area the horse trail forks. The trail to the west is a dead end trail going up near the divide to a view point. From there you can look down into Black Joe and Big Sandy Lakes on the other side. The main horse trail goes on north from Deep Creek Lakes over into the North Fork of Popo Agie River. Just before reaching it you'll join the Pinto Park Trail which goes back to the east, back to the Middle Fork Popo Agie River into Three Forks Park. However, the main use for this trail going across Deep Creek Lakes to the North Fork of Popo Agie is to turn up the North Fork and follow it up to Lonesome Lake inside the Cirque of the Towers. Hikers can go from Lonesome Lake up through Big Sandy Pass and back out to Big Sandy Openings. Also coming back this way from Big Sandy Lake you can go up Rapid Creek past Rapid, Miller and Temple Lakes and through the pass. Then come down Little Sandy Creek to Little Sandy Lake, take the Little Sandy Trail over and down Larson Creek back to your car at Sweetwater Entrance.

Only as man watches the unwary clouds drifting aimlessly, or gazes at the countless stars in his celestial surroundings, will he observe his real self. Until he can visualize himself as but one of the multitude of creatures roaming earth's crust, will he cast aside greed, love his fellowman, and live as God designed.

Finis Mitchell

LOUIS LAKE ENTRANCE

Trails: Louis Lake, Christina Lake

U.S.G.S. Maps: Christina Lake, Cony Mountain

The Louis Lake Trail which runs from Louis Lake to Christina Lake is little used by backpackers as they prefer the Forest Service trail coming from Fidders Lake.

LOUIS LAKE TRAIL

The Louis Lake Trail actually starts from Louis Lake and there is a good all-weather road going there. From the Wyoming 28 highway near Atlantic City you turn north onto the Louis Lake Road and it's about seven miles to the lake.

This Louis Lake Road goes all the way over to Lander, passing Louis, Fiddlers and Frye Lakes, past the Sinks in Sinks Canyon and is paved from there on to Lander. This is a beautiful scenic drive for people just out for a day in their car. You can start at either end, near Atlantic City or Lander and drive all the way, using Wyoming 28 to return to where you began. The Louis Lake trail starts at the Louis Lake Guard Station and goes up to Deer Park where it joins the old road going on to Gustave Lake and Christina Lake.

CHRISTINA LAKE TRAIL

Christina Lake Trail runs from Fiddler Lake across to Christina Lake with side trails going into Atlantic and Silas Canyons. The Louis Lake Trail is used mostly by

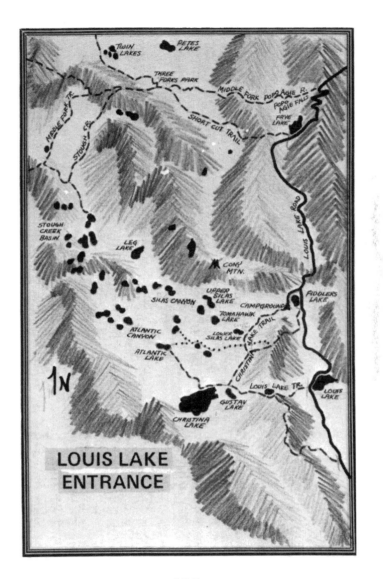

LOUIS LAKE
ENTRANCE

tourists and guests of the resort area around Louis Lake. Hikers and back packers will probablywant to drive on past Louis Lake over to Fiddlers Lake where the Forest Service has built the Christina Lake Trail over to Christina Lake. This trail begins at the Fiddler Lake Campground which is around on the other side from the main road. (Another trail begins where the main road first reaches the lake at its southeast corner. This trail crosses Fiddler Creek and Atlantic Creek and joins the Christina Lake Trail after about three miles.)

The Christina Lake Trail is about five miles long and goes over to Gustave Lake where it joins the old road going on to Christina Lake about a mile farther.

Atlantic Lake can be reached on a trail leading off from the road at the dam at the outlet of Christina Lake. It's about three miles to the first lake above in Atlantic Canyon. There are five more lakes above this one but the trail ends at the first one. The next large lake up the canyon has golden trout in it. All these lakes sit in beautiful glacial cirques with tall cliffs and peaks around them. You can make your way into most of them by just following up the stream. They are all above timberline so you can see all over the place.

Fishermen wanting to go to Atlantic Lake from Fiddlers Lake don't have to go all the way to Christina Lake then up to Atlantic. Starting on either trail at Fiddlers Lake they go until they come to Atlantic Creek. Stay on the north side and follow this creek all the way to Atlantic Lake. This route is two miles shorter. There is no trail on this route, you just follow the stream. About a mile before you get to Atlantic Lake, a stream comes in from the north and you can follow it up to two smaller lakes. There are nice brook trout in the lower one.

Silas Lakes and Tomahawk Lakes can be reached from the Christina Lake Trail. Before you get to Atlantic Creek on this trail from Fiddler Lake, you'll cross Silas Creek in a meadow. A sign here points up a trail going to Lower Silas Lake. From here you follow the streams up to Tomahawk Lake or to Upper Silas Lake depending on which stream you follow. Going on up stream about a mile you enter Silas Canyon which contains seven lakes and some good fishing. Lots of people fish up in here and it's a great trip into here from Fiddler Lake. It's about five miles up to the Canyon and another mile or so into the lakes. Silas Canyon is a glacial canyon, above timberline, with tall ledges, cliffs and granite rock formations around the cirques.

Within a wilderness if man but hesitates for a moment and as yet has not believed there is a God, it is time he take inventory of his soul and respect things more valuable than silver and gold.

Mans very existance lies within the earth. That is why our wilderness areas have been set aside, to keep him from exploiting all the earth. At every opportunity any area that qualifies should be added to it and preserved for coming generations.

Finis Mitchell

MIDDLE FORK ENTRANCE

Trails: Middle Fork, Shoshone, Pinto Park,
Stough Creek Basin

U.S.G.S. Maps: Cony Mountain, Sweetwater Gap

A trail from here is a short cut over to
the Middle Popo Agie River Trail which will
take you to the rivers headwaters where you
can go to Poison, Coon, and Toyo Lakes and
Wind River Peak. Side trails take you into
Deep Creek and Ice Lakes. Stough Creek Basin
Trail runs from below Three Forks Park up
into the Stough Creek Basin with its many
lakes. Pinto Park Trail branches off at
Three Forks Park and goes through Pinto Park
and on over into Sanford Park on the North
Popo Agie.

MIDDLE FORK TRAIL

The Middle Fork Trail actually starts
near the Bruce Campground above the Sinks on
the Louis Lake Road. (Horses start here).
For hikers it's far better to drive up the
switchbacks to higher country to Frye Lake.
This way you avoid much climbing and it's
several miles closer to the Primitive Area
Boundary.

To get to Frye Lake take the Louis Lake
Road out of Lander. From the center of
Lander, a paved road turns off U.S. 287 which
is Main Street and you'll see signs pointing
to the Sinks which is a winter sports area.
You'll drive right up Mid Popo Agie River to
the sinks. Here the river runs underground
through the rocks and comes up again on the

109

other side of the highway. You keep going on this road, up the switchbacks and on to Frye Lake.

One mile south of Frye Lake, and some six miles north of Fiddlers Lake on the Louis Lake Road, a big signboard faces traffic from either direction. It reads "Fremont County Youth Camp ½ mile", "Townsen Creek 1 mile", and "Worthen Meadows Reservoir 2 miles". One half mile past Townsen Creek, a small sign reads "Sheep Bridge Trail". It is a cutoff much shorter than from Frye Lake. The road ends at the west end of the reservoir. Near the end a small sign reads "Roaring Fork Lake ½ mile" on an old sheep wagon road, used only by truck and jeep.

At Roaring Fork Lake, one crosses the outlet on driftwood, and heads up the trail. This is a recent improvement, and you can't lose the trail. At about three miles (you'll think it's five) this trail reaches an open saddle right at timberline with a magnificient view of Wind River Peak 13,192 feet. Here it heads down into the timber, and later joins the trail from Bills Park and to Stough Creek Lakes.

However, from this saddle, an old Indian trail leads (if you can follow it) to the left, right at timberline around the mountain to a second saddle, from which it leads up a gradual slope to the west point of Roaring Fork Mountain. In this pass stands a monstrous cairn some ten feet high. From here you can see 11 of the Stough Creek Lakes directly in front of you. I left a note in a bottle in this cairn Sept. 14, 1975. If you find it, you know you've mastered the short route to the Stough Creek Lakes.

SHOSHONE TRAIL

Just a little ways up from Sheep Bridge on the Middle Popo Agie River this trail takes off to the right and goes over to Shoshone Lake about five miles away. There's nothing over there but fishing. The trail climbs steeply out of the canyon at the beginning but once on top, it's fairly easy hiking through the Hudson Meadows and into Shoshone Basin. If you wanted to go just to Shoshone Lake, a closer way would be to drive into Dickinson Park where a trail about four miles long goes over into Shoshone Lake. You could have someone drop you off in Dickinson Park then pick you up at Frye Lake.

Going on up the Middle Fork Trail from Sheep Bridge there's good fishing all the way up this river.

STOUGH CREEK BASIN TRAIL

About a mile and a half above Sheep Bridge on the Middle Popo Agie River, Stough Creek comes in from the south. The Stough Creek Basin Trail follows up this creek. It goes into forty two different lakes in the Stough Creek Basin and drainage. These lakes sit in a beautiful huge cirque surrounded on three sides by huge ledges and cliffs of the Roaring Mountains. There is good fishing for large brook trout. Last time I was in there they were four and a half pounders. Two years ago some of my friends came out of there with two pounders, so they're getting smaller. Another branch of the trail comes in from the upper end of Bills Park, farther up the Middle Popo Agie River.

Going on up the Middle Popo Agie River from where Stough Creek came in, you soon reach Three Forks Park.

PINTO PARK TRAIL

Near a long wide part of the river in Three Forks Park (has good fishing in it) the Pinto Park Trail takes off to the north (right). The trail climbs up away from the river, levels off somewhat and then climbs into Pinto Park. From here it goes down again to join the trail on the North Popo Agie River. This trail will take you up to the Cirque of the Towers or down to a road in Dickinson Park.

Going on up the Middle Popo Agie River above Three Forks Park you go through Gill Park and then Bill Park. One branch of the Stough Creek Basin Trail takes off to the left at the upper end of the meadow. A little over a mile further up the river and Tayo Creek enters from the right. The main trail goes on up the river then swings off to end at Sweetwater Gap. Going on over through the gap, the Sweetwater Gap Trail takes you down to the road near the Sweetwater Guard Station.

Back at Tayo Creek on the Middle Popo Agie River, two trails take off. One goes up Tayo Creek to Poison Lake near Wind River Peak. The other trail goes over to Ice Lakes, Deep Creek Lakes and on over to North Popo Agie River. All these trails and routes are described in the Sweetwater Gap section of this book.

God gives us beauty in flora and fauna
And sends us friends to share it;
He opens the door of nature so man
Can join us in soul and spirit.

Finis Mitchell

Lizzard Head Peak over Lizzard Head Lake
and Bear Lake

DICKINSON PARK ENTRANCE

Trails: North Popo Agie, Smith Lake, Shoshone
Lake, Lizard Head, Bears Ears, Washakie Trail,
High Meadow Creek

U.S.G.S. Maps: Lizard Head, Dickinson Park,
Moccasin Lake, Washakie Park, Mt. Bonneville,
Roberts Mountain.

Smith Lake Trail goes up to Smith Lake
and others in this cirque. A branch trail
goes over to High Meadow Lake. Bears Ear
Trail goes up to Valentine Lake for big
golden trout. Here you join the Washakie
Trail going past Washakie Lake to Washakie
Pass to the other side of the divide. Lizard
Head Trail crosses from upper North Popo Agie
to Bears Ears Trail near Cathedral Peak.
Another trail goes over past Squaw Lake to
join the Washakie Trail which runs from
Moccasin Lake up to Washakie Pass on the
Continental Divide. Hailey Pass can also be
reached by going from Valentine Lake over to
Grave Lake and on up to the pass.

On Highway 287 towards Yellowstone Park
from Lander you go 14 miles to Ft. Washakie.
One half mile before you reach Ft. Washakie
you turn left onto a paved road where there's
a filling station, store etc. This is the
Dickinson Park Road. It is paved for about
two miles, then is a good all-weather road
clear to Dickinson Park and on to Mocassin
Lake. It climbs and climbs over numerous
switchbacks clear to the top of the mountain
where a side road takes off and goes over
into Dickinson Park. The old road stays on
the left hand side of Dickinson Creek and
goes into the marshy head of the meadows. A
new road crosses the creek back where you go
into the guard station but you turn left just
after crossing the creek and stay on the

Mt. Hooker at left over Grave Lake

right side. This is a drier road and ends in
the meadows. A trail crosses the meadow from
here to a sign post at the southwest corner
of the park.

SMITH LAKE TRAIL

The trail going to the right from the
signpost mentioned above goes over to Smith
Lake and several others. It will take you
about two hours to get there, it's about four
or five miles. The trail is a little steep
in places but I'd say anyone can walk over
there in three hours. Above Smith Lake is
Cathedral, Middle, Cloverleaf, and Cook Lakes
all sitting in a spectacular cirque like eggs
in a giant birdsnest. Two lakes have
mackinaw and the rest have brook trout - all
good fishing. Middle, Cathedral, Cloverleaf
are on northwest inlets and Cooks on
Southwest.

HIGH MEADOW CREEK TRAIL

From the Smith Lake Trail after you cross Smith Creek, a trail cuts off to the southeast around a mountain and goes up High Meadow Creek. Or you can reach this trail from the North Popo Agie River Trail. Going up High Meadow Creek, the trail goes up to Cliff and High Meadow Lake and ends. The last time I was there both these lakes had beautiful cutthroat trout in them. These lakes sit in high glacial cirques at about 10,000 feet.

NORTH POPO AGIE TRAIL

Follow the road on the left side of Dickinson Park as a far as it goes and when it ends the trail starts. It goes up out of the park to the southeast and climbs over the mountain and comes down into the North Fork of Popo Agie River. (Right here a trail crosses the river and climbs up to Shoshone Lake where there's good fishing.)

Going up the river in a mile or so you'll cross the mouth of Smith Creek. Another mile or so and you'll reach High Meadow Creek and cross it. A trail goes up this creek to High Meadow Lake, described earlier. You continue on up through Sanford Park where at the upper end trails come in from Pinto Park and Deep Creek Lakes. These trails are described in the Middle Fork Section of this book.

You continue climbing gradually up the river to Lizard Head Meadows and then on to Lonesome Lake in the Cirque of the Towers. From Lizard Head Meadows on up, the two tallest peaks on your left are Dog Tooth and then Mitchell Peak.

Dog Tooth Peak above Papoose Lake

CIRQUE OF THE TOWERS

Surrounding Lonesome Lake at 10,187 feet on three sides are tall peaks that make up the famous Cirque of the Towers. They are all over 12,000 feet, from War Bonnet at 12,406 on the southwest and Lizard Head at 12,842 to the northeast. All these peaks are on the Continental Divide with falling raindrops splitting, half going to the Atlantic Ocean to the east and half going to the Pacific Ocean to the west. This area is a heaven for mountain climbers as you can camp in the cirque and climb different peaks for days on end. A trail takes off to the south from Lonesome Lake and climbs over to Arrowhead Lake and on down to the Big Sandy Openings. Another route goes north (no

117

trail) over into Texas Lake, down Washakie
Creek to Marms and Dads Lakes, and on to the
Big Sandy Openings Campground. Both these
routes are described in more detail in the
Big Sandy Openings section of this book. The
Big Sandy route is only about ten miles into
the cirque so is a closer route than coming
up the North Popo Agie Trail. It's probably
fourteen miles coming up from Dickinson Park.

LIZARD HEAD TRAIL

A lot of people don't like to return by
the same trail and at Lizard Head Meadows a
loop trail begins that will take you back to
Dickinson Park. A ways below where the
stream comes down from Bear Lake into Lizard
Head Meadows, the trail takes off to the
north. It climbs quite steeply out onto an
old glacial plateau above Bear Lake. From
here you just follow the trail which is
fairly level, maybe going down some clear
over to and around Cathedral Peak. Here it
joins the Bears Ears Trail which goes over to
join the Washakie Trail to the left, or to
the right it goes around Mt. Chauvenet and
Bears Ears Mountain and back down to
Dickinson Park, about eight miles from
Cathedral Peak.

BEARS EARS TRAIL

This trail runs from below Dickinson Park
over to Valentine Lake where the largest
California Golden Trout in the Wind Rivers
are found today. You take the road that goes
over to the North Fork Guard Station and the
trail begins a ways up the road to the right
after crossing Dickinson Creek. You cross

DICKINSON PARK ENTRANCE

119

Ranger Creek right at the beginning and then climb steadily for about three miles. For another five miles it's up and down a few hundred feet, past Bears Ears Mountain and Mt. Chauvenet and over below Cathedral Peak. Here the trail forks, the left branch going on around Cathedral Peak and on across the glacial plateau and down to join the North Popo Agie Trail which returns to Dickinson Park. The Bears Ears Trail goes down (right) from the trail junction to Valentine Lake where it joins the Washakie Trail. The Goldens in Valentine Lake are large and fat and difficult to catch. Evidently there is plenty to eat in the lake so they are tough to get hold of.

At Valentine Lake you can go west on the Washakie Trail to Washakie Lake and on to Washakie Pass. Going northeast on the Washakie trail you can go down to Mocassin Lake on the Indian Reservation or swing around past Squaw Lake and back to Dickinson Park. A rock slide has blocked the Washakie Trail between Moss and Dutch Oven Lakes.

WASHAKIE TRAIL

This trail starts at Mocassin Lake at the end of the Mocassin Lake - Dickinson Park road. The beginning is on the Indian Reservation so you must have a permit from the Indians to use this area. The trail runs up past Valentine and Washakie Lakes to Washakie Pass on the Continental Divide.

A trail from Dickinson Park goes over and joins the Washakie Trail near Squaw Lake. It starts near the old North Fork Guard Station up the road that crosses Dickinson Creek about a mile after you leave the Mocassin Lake Road. The trail goes north into the Reservation and on to Hobbs Park. A branch

Big Chief Mt. reflected in Valentine Lake

trail comes up from another Ranger Station in Mosquito Park just off the Mocassin Lake Road. Continuing on through Hobbs Park you climb to a pass below Mt. Cross then descend to Squaw Lake. About a mile beyond this lake you'll join the Washakie Trail. The Washakie Trail and this section coming over from Dickinson Park goes around all the mountains that the Bears Ears Trail goes over.

On the Washakie Trail you climb for about two miles to Gaylord Lake where there are no fish. About a mile further you'll reach Moss Lake which sits in an extremely deep cirque. The trail crosses the stream at the outlet of the lake and then branches. The right fork is the best route if you're heading for Grave Lake (mackinaw trout) and Hailey Pass. The trail goes around Valentine Mountain, down to cross the South Fork Little Wind River, then right up a mile and a half to Grave Lake. It's about three steep miles farther to Hailey Pass on the divide at 11,169 feet.

The left fork at Moss Lake is the main Washakie Trail and climbs steeply up the stream and crosses over and goes past Dutch Oven Lake and down to Valentine Lake. The Bears Ears Trail joins from the left before you get down to the lake. From Valentine Lake the trail goes down to the South Fork Little Wind River. You may have a little trouble crossing there. You might have to take off your boots and wade. After you cross, there are three sign boards. A side trail goes down the river about a mile and a half, then goes up to Grave Lake and on to Hailey Pass. The Washakie Trail climbs up to reach Washakie Lake in about a mile.

In Washakie Lake there are large hybrid trout. They are a cross between golden and rainbow trout. The reason they are so large is because they don't reproduce. Both kinds of trout are spring spawners. Both like the same places and water temperature to spawn in, so there are a lot of hybrid trout as a result.

North of Washakie Lake, off the trail where you can't see it is another lake where we planted German browns and they are still there. They can't get away, that's why we put them there because they eat other fish.

Going on, the trail crosses the outlet of Macon Lake (nice brook trout) and climbs a mile further to Washakie Pass. Along here, you will find big snowdrifts until late August. The snow is solid so it presents no problem for hiker or horse. Be careful not to step near a protruding rock as the snow melts next to the rock and you'll slide down and hurt your ankle or knee.

Washakie Peak can be easily climbed from the pass. Come down the trail on the west side a little ways and stay just under the pinnacles to the right of some sawtooth points and you can walk all the way to the summit. The east side is all cliffs but on the west side you can make it easy. At the top at 12,524 feet you can see in all directions. The Cirque of the Towers stick up like a bunch of needles to the southeast. Just short of them you can see Billy and Shadow Lakes on Washakie Creek.

From the pass, Washakie Trail continues on over and down the other side past Skull Lake, crosses Washakie Creek and joins the Highline Trail at Marms Lake described earlier in Big Sandy Entrance.

A beautiful loop trail can be made from Big Sandy Openings and a lot of hikers do it. Go up the Big Sandy Trail, up North Creek into the Cirque of the Towers, down to Lizard Head Meadows, up Lizard Head Trail and down to Valentine Lake. Go either way to Grave Lake and Hailey Pass or Washakie Lake and Washakie Pass, back down to Marms Lake and the Highline Trail back to Big Sandy Openings. This loop would take at least four days and a week would be better.

(The Washakie Creek on the west side has nothing to do with the Washakie Trail which is mostly on the east side of the divide.)

However, if you have a permit to hike on the Indian Reservation, just east of where Grave Creek enters Grave Lake on the north side, a trail leaves the lake and leads down to Onion Meadows. After crossing Raft Creek a right turn also crosses Lost Creek, passes Vernal Lake, takes up Moss Creek to join the Washakie Trail at Moss Lake, hence, back to Moccasin Lake at end of road.

Now back at Onion Meadows you turn left

back up Raft Creek, follow up to a nice
saddle (pass) and down Twenty Lakes Creek
near big Raft Lake and the trail turns back
west to join the main trail on North Fork
Little Wind River a half mile above Movo
Lake, out of St. Lawrence Basin, next
Entrance in this book.

ST. LAWRENCE BASIN ENTRANCE

Trails: St. Lawrence Creek, South Fork,
North Fork of Little Wind River

U.S.G.S. Maps: St. Lawrence Basin, Paradise
Basin

The South Fork Trail goes over into the
head of North Fork of Little Wind River to
many lakes above Raft Lake. Also to 14 lakes
on Twenty Lakes Creek, south inlet to Raft
Lake. St. Lawrence Creek Trail goes over
into the headwaters of Bull Lake Creek and
through Windy Gap into the South Fork and
Alpine Lakes country.

This area is on the Wind River Indian
Reservation so a permit to enter must be
obtained.

The trails begin near the St. Lawrence
Ranger Station. To get there you drive north
from Ft. Washakie eight miles on U.S. 287
and turn west onto the St. Lawrence Ranger
Station Road (Sage Creek Road). The station
is about 18 miles up at the end of this road.

At the road end near the station two
trails take off and begin as jeep roads.
Better park your car near the station and
start hiking. The South Fork Trail goes up
to the Wilson Creek Lakes and also down to

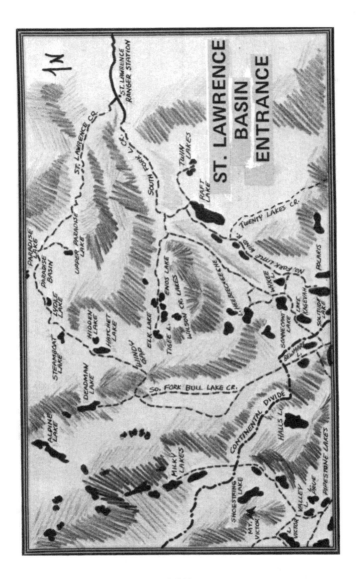

ST. LAWRENCE BASIN ENTRANCE

the Raft Lake Country. The St. Lawrence Creek Trail runs over to Paradise Basin and on over to the South Fork of Bull Lake Creek.

ST. LAWRENCE CREEK TRAIL

This is the high route taking off to the right from the ranger station. The jeep road runs about a quarter mile then the trail continues to climb gradually to the head of the creek. You climb some more and pass through a saddle and start down into Paradise Basin.

Paradise Basin is a high mostly open basin with Paradise Creek running through it and Paradise Lakes are on the far side. Just as you enter the basin coming out of the trees a trail crosses and if you follow it back to the left about a mile and a half you'll reach Upper Paradise Lake. All these lakes used to be the hottest fishing and I think they're still pretty good for rainbow trout.

The trail that crossed back in the basin comes up into the basin from the Bull Lake Country to the northeast of here.

The basin is about a mile and a half across then you go about a mile up to Lydle Lake which is on Sheep Creek. Another two miles and you pass Steamboat Lake. Another mile and you cross Hatchet Creek and follow it up to Hatchet Lake, a mile further. I don't know if we ever had any fish in Hidden Lake which is just over the hump to the east from Hatchet Lake.

Continuing on from Hatchet Lake you climb steeply over some switchbacks up to Windy Gap which is a low pass on Windy Ridge. Then you descend about two thousand feet elevation in a mile and a half to the South Fork Bull Lake Creek. The only reason to go down there is because it's hot fishing. When you reach the creek, you'll join a trail coming down the stream from the pass going across the divide to Bewmark and Middle Fork Lakes on the other side. You follow down the trail to Deadman Lake and that's as far as a horse can go. This is where it's real good fishing. You'll probably want to spend several days in this area. You can hike on downstream past another lake and on to Bull Lake Creek. Here turn left and go up the creek about a mile to Alpine Lake which is about a mile and a half long and good fishing. Other lakes are on up the creek and if you have time you can get over into the Milky Lakes area.

SOUTH FORK TRAIL

This begins as a jeep road and runs for about a mile and the trail continues. You cross the creek and follow up the west side to the Meadows at the head of the stream. Then you climb about a mile to a low saddle and cross over into the Entigo and Wilson Creek drainages which both run into Raft Lake. Two trails go south along here and will be described further on.

Continuing west you cross Entigo Creek and go on about a mile further to Wilson Creek. Going up Wilson Creek you encounter a whole series of Wilson Creek Lakes. You'll go past Enos, Tigee and end at Elk Lake in a huge cirque below Horse Mountain. All these lakes are good fishing.

NORTH FORK OF LITTLE WIND RIVER TRAIL

Back at Entigo Creek the trail going south goes down to Raft Lake and up the North Fork of Little Wind River. A fork in the trail above Raft Lake takes off to the east and crosses over to Twin Lakes on Twenty Lakes Creek. The other branch stays above the lake and goes southwest to Movo Lake and on up North Fork Little Wind River past several smaller lakes to Wykee Lake. Going on, you climb on up the trail to where it ends at Lake Solitude at 10,522 feet. There are several more lakes above this one which you can find your way to. All these lakes are such good fishing that after awhile you'll just want to explore around just for the sheer enjoyment of seeing this high country.

Back at Wilson Creek at the lower end of the lakes another trail goes south parallel to the other trail but stays up high above the river. It continues southwest with a branch going over to Lake Heebeecheeche on Glacier Creek. There are several good-sized lakes upstream from this one that you can find your way to. Going on you come to Sonnecant Lake. Here an old trail goes on up past Lake Kagevah and on up over the divide to Bewmark and Middle Fork Lakes on the other side, described in Scab Creek Entrance. This trail is blocked for horses because of rock slides. Also at Sonnecant Lake a trail goes down to Wykee Lake from southeast corner of Sonnecant Lake to inlet of Wykee Lake to join the North Fork Little Wind River Trail.

East face of Gannett Peak from Mt. Teffas

BURRIS ENTRANCE

Trails: Ink Wells Trail, Dry Creek Trail,
Horse Ridge Route

U.S.G.S. Maps: Hays Park, Ink Wells, Fremont
Peak No., Gannett Peak

Ink Wells Trail goes through Scenic Pass
into the Ink Wells Lakes and connects with
the Glacier Trail which goes up to Gannett
Peak. A side route is the Horse Ridge Route
which is a very scenic hiking route all along
Horse Ridge, no trail. Dry Creek Trail runs
over to the headwaters of Dry Creek
containing many lakes enclosed by Horse and
Dry Creek Ridges.

This is one route to Gannett Peak but is not used much anymore. It crosses Indian land and a permit must be obtained before using it.

The trail starts at Cold Springs which is at the end of a road coming in from Burris on U.S. 287. Burris consists of a small house with a store, at one time had a post office also. You go about a mile and a quarter on up the highway northwest beyond Burris and turn off to the left onto the Cold Springs Road (called Gannett Peak Road on U.S.G.S. maps). A branch of this road goes to the Hidden Valley Guest Ranch and Indians are requiring permits to use either of the roads. A jeep or four-wheel drive is needed to use this entry road.

The road goes up Little Dry Fork, staying on the north side until further in. The Hidden Valley road branches off to the left, crossing the stream after about three miles but you don't take that road. You drive on up to Cold Springs which is about ten miles from the highway. You park your car and put your Indian permit (one for each person) in the window so it can be seen. The Indians patrol this area so be sure you have a permit.

Starting up the trail, you'll hike about a mile to the edge of Hays Park where the trail forks. The Ink Wells Trail goes to the right on to Gannett Peak. The Dry Creek Trail turns left and goes over into some good fishing country along Dry Creek which has fifty lakes on it.

DRY CREEK TRAIL

Shortly after branching onto this trail in Hays Park you cross the Reservation Boundary and go off the Indian Land. You climb gradually aways around the side of a mountain and then begin your descent down to Phillips Lake. This is the beginning of a series of lakes along Dry Creek and its branches that has been some of the best fishing in the Wind Rivers.

Upstream from Phillips Lake is Grassy Lake with two smaller lakes above it on a side stream. Next to it is Native Lake where on the far side the trail divides. The right branch goes up a side creek to Moose, Cub, Don Lakes and many unnamed lakes above them. The other branch of the trail goes up Dry Creek to another group of lakes. These two trails go into branches of one giant cirque surrounded by Horse Ridge on the west and Dry Ridge on the east. It's all hot fishing in here and spectacular country to explore. Both trails end in these cirques.

INK WELLS TRAIL

This trail leading in to the Ink Wells Lakes and on to Gannett Peak branches to the right at its beginning in Hays Park above Cold Springs. It starts climbing right from the beginning and goes up about 1,600 feet in three and a half miles to Scenic Pass on Horse Ridge. The trail goes down to the lakes where there are brook trout. But the original trail took off to the left higher up and stayed above the lakes to join the other trail beyond the lakes.

Echo Lake is about a mile further past Ink Wells Lakes on the trail. Just past here

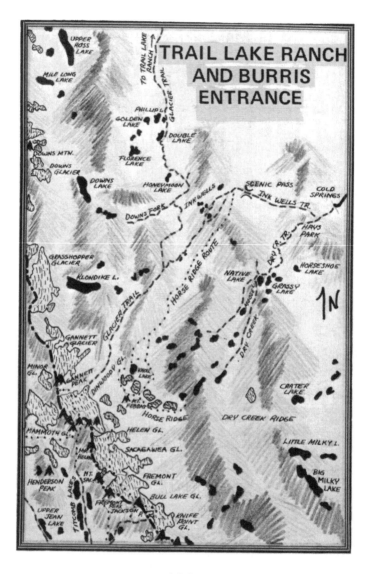

TRAIL LAKE RANCH AND BURRIS ENTRANCE

you'll start down for about a mile and a half
and join the Glacier Trail which runs on to
Gannett Peak and starts at Trail Lake Ranch
near Dubois. There's a good footbridge to
cross the stream from one rock wall to the
other to get on the main trail on the other
side.

(For the rest of this route to Gannett
Peak, see the Trail Lake Ranch Entrance
description which covers the entire Glacier
Trail.)

HORSE RIDGE ROUTE

This is a very scenic route going along
Horse Ridge south from Scenic Pass on the Ink
Wells Trail. It is an easy route to follow
as it stays on top the ridge and you can't
get off anywhere. There is no trail and none
is needed, you just wander wherever you wish
from side to side as you look into the many
lakes, cirques and glaciers below on both
sides. This route is for hikers that just
want to see beautiful country. There is
plenty of water up here, springs, boggy
places and a lake. This route runs for about
ten miles, clear to the south end of the
ridge. You're walking at about 12,000 feet
all along the route.

Knoll Lake (no fish) is a large lake on
the ridge at 12,165 feet. When I named it, I
meant the name to be Noel but it came out
Knoll on the maps. There are no trees or
special camping places here but you can throw
down your sleeping bag anywhere on the ridge.
There are steep glaciers on the south side of
the lake.

Passing above the lake you'll climb to
above 13,000 feet and walk over the glacier
near Chimney Rock. Don't go out on Chimney

Rock as it's unsafe, nothing but a pile of junk - broken slabs that are continually falling off and piling up below.

Mt. Febbas at 13,468 feet is nearby due west of Chimny Rock and easily reached. From there you'll look almost straight west to Gannett Peak and countless glaciers along the east side of the divide. (Many of these glaciers and Gannett Peak can also be seen from back along the ridge.)

Horse Ridge swings around to the east, drops a little lower and you can walk right on out to the end. Here you are overlooking Indian Pass and can see across to Dry Creek Ridge beyond. There is no way off though, so you must turn around and go back to the Ink Wells Trail for your return trip.

I intend to take my whole family with the grandkids and their mothers, just as soon as the little ones are old enough, (five or six years old or in school) and bring them up here. We'll spend a whole week showing them mountains, glaciers and lakes and show them how to take care of themselves in a glacial wilderness.

In wilderness man steps into isolationism, into solace and tranquility. Perhaps he'll see no human being except himself. He'll be trespassing in wildlife's domain. He'll be an integral part of nature. He'll speak the language of the mountain, of it's inhabitants. He'll live as God designed. He'll recognize earth's ecosystem as sustenance for both fauna and flora, God's most rewarding gift to man.

Finis Mitchell

The Glacier Trail up Dinwoody River;
Gannett Peak at left

TRAIL LAKE RANCH ENTRANCE

Trails: Glacier Trail

U.S.G.S. Maps: Torrey Lake, Ink Wells,
Fremont Peak No., Gannett Peak

    Glacier Trail is the main northern route
to Gannett Peak. It goes over into Dinwoody
Canyon,joins the Ink Wells Trail from Burris
and the two go on up Dinwoody Creek to the
Dinwoody Glacier moraines and definitely
ends, but the route continues on to Gannett
Peak and/or to Dinwoody Pass.
    Probably 80 percent of all climbers and
glacier seekers going to Gannett Peak use the

Glacier Trail. This starts at Trail Lake Ranch near Torrey Lake. To get there go three miles east of Dubois on U.S. 287 just across the bridge on Jakeys Fork. A road turns off to the right at a cattle guard going to the state fish hatchery. You stay on the left road after crossing the cattle guard. It's a graded dirt road and gets pretty rocky as you near the end of it. You drive to the end of the road and come to the Trail Lake Ranch which is an extension of the Wyoming University. The road ends above the buildings where you can park your car. There is one table and a toilet there.

GLACIER TRAIL

To get on Glacier Trail, you go down in the willows from where you parked your car and look for a log bridge crossing Torrey Creek. Across this bridge you'll see a sign saying there is no water for ten miles on this Glacier Trail.

You'll climb up through trees for about an hour and a half then you get above the timber. You're hiking along an old glacier bed plateau as you gradually climb on up to a low saddle at 10,895 feet. Here you'll start down into Burrow Flat where the Dinwoody Trail joins from the east. There is a signboard at this junction. This trail goes down to Phillips Ranch at Dinwoody Lakes, and is seldom used by hikers.

You descend to Phillips Lake on Phillips Creek. Here is where the poor trail begins. You come down in here and wind around, climbing up and down. It's a clear trail, you can't get off it as it goes on past Double Lake and Star Lake. There is water everywhere from here on, only the first part of the trail is it advisable to carry a canteen full. Along these lakes there are plenty of places to camp and it's good fishing.

From Star down to Honeymoon Lake you go back and forth through sliced ledges to get there. A lot of people come here and camp to fish and pick huckleberries. The trail goes on down the stream from the lake for about a mile where a side trail cuts off to the left to go over to a falls (a sign here) on Dinwoody Creek. These falls are worth seeing if you have the time.

The trail reaches Downs Fork Meadows on Dinwoody Creek and you will have to follow the trail to the upper end of the meadows to get across Downs Fork on a bridge. This is all prime moose country and you may see them along here. At the bridge you'll see a sign. The trail up Downs Fork is a horse trail used only by hunters. The water coming down this creek is coming from Downs and Grasshopper Glaciers. The trail goes up this fork only a couple of miles and stops.

Cross the bridge and follow the trail on up Dinwoody River for many miles. After about four miles the Ink Wells Trail joins from the left. You go on another 10 miles through Wilson Meadows, past the mouth of Gannett Creek that comes down from Gannett Glacier at right. Hold right and cross Gannett Creek in 5 channels, then back to Dinwoody River up trail to timberline.

The Glacier Trail continues on up Dinwoody River right up to the end of the valley and stops as you reach the huge rocks of the glacial moraine at the lower face of Dinwoody Glacier. From here you follow on up the stream and it's best to stay on the snow as much as possible to avoid the rocks. On the snow stay away from rocks sticking up through, as the snow melts around the rocks forming openings that you can fall into and scrape your leg on the rock, and may break a leg.

Stay on the snow going up until you get onto the ice of the glacier itself. It's advisable to use crampons, a rope and ice axes from here on up. You can see Gannett Peak at the right and many others ahead of you. Gannett is white-capped with ice all over the summit so you can't miss it. You climb up the main body of the glacier going around to the south side of Gooseneck Pinnacle and about even with the next pinnacle to the south of it. Actually you're looking at Glacier Pass ahead of you but you can't go on up to it because that finger of the glacier is full of crevasses. So you turn north and climb onto the east prong of Gooseneck Pinnacle. Here you'll find some camping places among the rocks on the ridge, spots for two alpine tents, walled up with rocks to hold tents against the winds. I left them there August 7 and 8, 1974. Water 15 feet from tents on Gooseneck Glacier.

From the camping place about a third of the way up Gooseneck Pinnacle you are a whole day up to the top of Gannett Peak and back. Some people camp back at the edge of the moraine but it's an hour or so up to the higher place so it would be a longer day to get to the summit and back. I camped at the moraines in 1973 and got back to camp at 12:30 A.M. Also, if you're going out by way of Titcomb Basin it's better to camp on the pinnacle ridge.

Next morning you walk over to the ice, put on your crampons, rope up, take your ice axe and start climbing. You climb along the south side of Gooseneck Glacier until you get next to the tall pinnacle itself and then

138

On Dinwoody Glacier; Mt. Warren left,
Doublet Peak, and Dinwoody Peak

climb back onto the rocks again. There will
be crevasses and burgshrungs where the ice
separates from the cliffs. These are
dangerous and should be carefully avoided.
Your ropes are used in case you slip into
one.

When you climb back onto the rocks you
take off your crampons but remain tied into
your rope. You climb right on up the rocky
ridge and soon reach the Continental Divide
and you're on Summit Ridge. There is a
thousand foot wall of ice on one side of the
ridge and it's better to stay on the rocks to
the left of it as you go on up the ridge
approaching the summit. Soon you'll be right
on the brink where there isn't room to walk
on the rocks so you'll go onto the snow.

It's a little bit level on top so you can walk on over to the summit on the snow. When you get there you'll think that you've conquered the world. You're at 13,804, the highest point in Wyoming. It probably took four hours to get there from the high camp and you'll probably waste an hour and a half looking and taking pictures from the top. There is a copper tube like a stove pipe with a hinged cap that contains a big rolled-up registration book that you'll want to sign.

Going back down in 1974, we had to lay over in our camp an extra night because the wind was blowing so hard you could hardly stand up. We got out of the tent and piled rocks to form a wall around the south and west sides of our tents because the wind tore our ropes out three times. The third time we gave it up and built the walls.

Next morning we roped up again, put on our crampons and headed for Dinwoody Pass, as we weren't going to go back on the Glacier Trail. First we crossed the ice below Glacier Pass and followed the ice rim around the huge buttress to the south. The layers in the ice rim represents hundreds of years of snow-fall on the glacier where you can take pictures of it. You climb on up the glacier as high as you can towards Dinwoody Pass to the south. There are a lot of broken chunks and crevasses but you stay roped together and go around all this stuff. When you have climbed as high as you can, you step over onto the rocks and take off the crampons and rope. From here you just make your way up the rocks to the pass. Just as you reach the pass there's a spring under a big rock off to the west a ways where you can get water any time of the year.

Dinwoody Peak can easily be hiked to from the pass. You drop your packs at the pass

and head right up the mountain, to the east.
It doesn't get nasty until just as you reach
the tip of the point but you can always walk
around between the rocks to the top. This is
a great picture spot to view all the glaciers
and peaks on all sides. You can't go on
along the divide from here so you return to
your pack in the pass.

Most climbers going only to Gannett Peak
will probably come in on the Glacier Trail.
If they plan to do a lot of other climbing
they'll probably come up Titcomb Basin from
Elkhart Park Entrance. Probably the closest
and best way would be from Elkhart Park. You
can set up camp in upper Titcomb Basin in
two days coming from Elkhart Park. But there
aren't very many who can go from upper
Titcomb Lake, over Dinwoody Pass and up to
Gannett Peak and back in one day. You
probably should take your sleeping bag on up
to Dinwoody Pass in the morning and then stay
there that night after climbing Gannett.

Bull Lake Glacier; Fremont Peak left, Sacagawea
Peak, Helen Peak right.

MY PLEDGE TO FUTURE GENERATIONS

While here on earth, I shall endeavor with all my ability and steadfast efforts to preserve and add to our wilderness so all who follow in my footsteps might have the same opportunity to use and enjoy it as I have. Remember, the way of a wilderness is love and kindness toward all forms of life.

Finis Mitchell

Back cover: Mitchell Peak 12,482 feet high.

Below: Bronze plaque mounted on Mitchell Peak

"MY THOUGHTS"

This is my home, but everybody's land.

Where man is so small and insignificant, the world knows not of his presence.

The land closest to Heaven is that where men love and respect all forms of life.

To fully enjoy life, we must help others to do likewise.

Man's tenure here is so destructive to the ecosystem of earth it can only lead to extinction of all.

Man should love the land and all it's wildlife as he does himself.

Man's failure to see when he looks can result only in self-destruction.

If man continues to exploit earth, not only will he vanish from malnutrition, but the earth shall die also.

This is not a cruel world, we need only to replace greed, graft, and corruption with love and kindness toward others of our own kind.

If you like my thoughts, show them to others, if not, show me my mistakes that I might correct them.

Finis Mitchell

"A MOUNTAIN MAN"

He who labors to reach the summit of a mountain seeks solace and tranquility. He is neither greedy nor selfish. He finds time to help others less fortunate than himself. He loves the great outdoors and all forms of life; the trees, the flowers, the grasses of the land and the land itself. He loves the music of cataracts from glacier to sea. He also loves the peace and quiet when life-giving streams linger momentarily in valley or lake along their way. He makes happy tracks in many snows which melt away, leaving no trace of man's visit to the wilderness. He finds time to do everything needful by never letting time find him doing nothing. He is a man among men.

He awakens always facing the East from whence the sun gives life to all things. As the day advances, he strives to help others attain greater heights from North to South. When the day is done he faces the West as the setting sun beckons him into peaceful slumber and puts the world to rest. He is thankful the earth provides his existance and for the priviledge of just being here; thankful to be on the summit of a mountain which shall stand forever as a sanctuary to God and man.

For him, may the winds that blow his way be always mild and the rains that fall upon him be warm and gentle. May the path he selects to follow through life be decorated with lilacs so the beauty and fragrance of the land be with him all the days of his life. May God be with him along his way and guide him through the darkest nights. Amen.

Finis Mitchell
422 M Street
Rock Springs, Wyo. 82901